ROUND THE CLOCK

ROUND THE CLOCK

THE EXPERIENCE OF
THE ALLIED BOMBER
CREWS WHO FLEW
BY DAY AND BY NIGHT
FROM ENGLAND IN THE
SECOND WORLD WAR

PHILIP KAPLAN
JACK CURRIE

For Margaret and Kate

First published in the United Kingdom in 1993 by
Cassell

This paperback edition first published in 2001 by
Cassell Paperbacks, Cassell & Co
Wellington House, 125 Strand
London, WC2R 0BB

Text copyright © Philip Kaplan, 1993
Page 231 is an extension of this copyright notice

Distributed in the United States of America by
Sterling Publishing Co., Inc.
387 Park Avenue South,
New York, NY 10016-8810

A CIP catalogue record for this book is available
from the British Library

ISBN 1-84188-128-7

Printed in China through Colorcraft Ltd. Hong Kong

CASSELLPAPERBACKS

CONTENTS

UNITED STATES ARMY AIR
FORCE AND ROYAL AIR FORCE
BOMBER STATIONS IN
WORLD WAR II ENGLAND

HEADQUARTERS ORGANIZATIONS-USAAF
BRAMPTON GRANGE-1ST WING HQ
KETTERINGHAM HALL-2ND WING HQ
ELVEDEN HALL-3RD WING HQ
MARKS HALL-4TH WING HQ
STISTED HALL-5TH WING HQ

HEADQUARTERS ORGANIZATIONS-RAF
BAWTRY-1 GROUP HQ
EXNING-3 GROUP HQ
YORK-4 GROUP HQ
SWINDERBY-5 GROUP HQ
ALLERTON-6 GROUP (RCAF) HQ
HUNTINGDON 8 GROUP (PFF) HQ
ABINGDON-91 GROUP (OTU) HQ
WINSLOW-92 GROUP (OTU) HQ
EGGINTON-93 GROUP (OTU) HQ
BYLAUGH HALL-100 GROUP HQ

MIDDLETON ST GEORGE
CROFT
LEEMING
SKIPTON-ON-SWALE
WOMBLETON
TOPCLIFFE
DISHFORTH
DALTON
THOLTHORPE
LINTON-ON-OUSE
EAST MOOR
DRIFFIELD
FULL SUTTON
LISSET
ALLERTON
MARSTON MOOR
YORK
RUFFORTH
POCKLINGTON
ELVINGTON
LECONFIELD
MELBOURNE
RICCALL
HOLME
HULL
LEEDS
BURN
BREIGHTON
SNAITH
NORTH KILLINGHOLME
ELSHAM WOLDS
SANDTOFT
KIRMINGTON
LINDHOLME
WALTHAM
FINNINGLEY
BLYTON
BINBROOK
SHEFFIELD
BIRCOTES
BAWTRY
KELSTERN
HEMSWELL
LUDFORD MAGNA
FALDINGWORTH
WICKENBY
WORKSOP
SCAMPTON
GAMSTON
DUNHOLME LODGE
LINCOLN
SKELLINGTHORPE
FISKERTON
SPILSBY
EAST KIRKBY
BARDNEY
WIGSLEY
WADDINGTON
METHERINGHAM
WOODHALL SPA
OSSINGTON
SWINDERBY
WINTHORPE
FULBECK
CONINGSBY
SYERSTON
BOTTESFORD
LANGAR
CHURCH BROUGHTON
EGGINTON
HIXON
CASTLE DONINGTON
SEIGHFORD
WYMESWOLD
PEPLOW
LICHFIELD
LEICESTER
WOOLFOX LODGE
NORTH LUFFENHAM
PETERBOROUGH
POLEBROOK
BRUNTINGTHORPE
DEENETHORPE
GLATTON
MARKET HARBOROUGH
UPWOOD
BITTESWELL
DESBOROUGH
WARBOYS
HUSBANDS BOSWORTH
HARRINGTON
MEPAL
WYTON
GRAFTON UNDERWOOD
ALCONBURY
WITCHFORD
HUNTINGDON
WATERBEACH
MOLESWORTH
BRAMPTON GRANGE
EXNING
CHELVESTON
GRAVELY
CAMBRIDGE
LITTLE STAUGHTON
KIMBOLTON
OAKINGTON
PODINGTON
THURLEIGH
BOURN
WELLESBOURNE MOUNTFORD
GAYDON
BEDFORD
TEMPSFORD
LONG MARSTON
CHIPPING WARDEN
GRANSDEN LODGE
STRATFORD
SILVERSTONE
HONEYBOURNE
TURWESTON
EDGEHILL
LITTLE HORWOOD
MORETON-IN-THE-MARSH
BARFORD ST JOHN
WINSLOW
WING
UPPER HEYFORD
WESTCOTT
ENSTONE
OAKLEY
STANTON HARCOURT
OXFORD
ABINGDON
HIGH WYCOMBE
LONDON

NORTH CREAKE
LITTLE SNORING
OULTON
FOULSHAM
GREAT MASSINGHAM
SWANNINGTON
WEST RAYNHAM
BYLAUGH HALL
MARHAM
SWANTON MORLEY
ATTLEBRIDGE
HORSHAM ST FAITH
DOWNHAM MARKET
WENDLING
RACKHEATH
NORWICH
NORTH PICKENHAM
SHIPDHAM
KETTERINGHAM HALL
BODNEY
HETHEL
GREAT YARMOUTH
METHWOLD
WATTON
DEOPHAM GREEN
HARDWICK
SEETHING
FELTWELL
EAST WRETHAM
OLD BUCKENHAM
BUNGAY
SNETTERTON HEATH
TIBENHAM
BECCLES
ELVEDEN HALL
THORPE ABBOTTS
MILDENHALL
KNETTISHALL
EYE
METFIELD
HONINGTON
HORHAM
HALESWORTH
TUDDENHAM
HEPWORTH
BURY ST EDMUNDS
MENDLESHAM
FRAMLINGHAM
NEWMARKET HEATH
GREAT ASHFIELD
RATTLESDEN
BUTLEY
CHEDBURGH
LAVENHAM
DEBACH
STRADISHALL
IPSWICH
WRATTING COMMON
SUDBURY
HADSTOCK
WATTISHAM
RAYDON
BASSINGBOURN
STEEPLE MORDEN
RIDGEWELL
WORMINGFORD
NUTHAMPSTEAD
WETHERSFIELD
BOXTED
GOSFIELD
EARLS COLNE
STANSTED
GREAT SALING
RIVENHALL
GREAT DUNMOW
MARKS HALL
BIRCH
MATCHING
BOREHAM
STISTED HALL
CHIPPING ONGAR

0   10   20   30   40   50   MILES

KEY: GREEN DOT=USAAF BASE   BLUE DOT=RAF BASE

ROUND THE CLOCK

DOING IT IN BROAD DAYLIGHT

The world is like a board with holes in it, and the square men have got into the round holes, and the round into the square.

—Bishop Berkeley

The strategic air offensive is a means of direct attack on the enemy state with the object of depriving it of the means or will to continue the war. It may in itself be the instrument of victory, or it may be the means by which victory can be won by other forces. It differs from all previous kinds of armed attack in that it alone can be brought to bear immediately, directly and destructively against the heartland of the enemy.

—The British Air Staff

IN 1942, when Brigadier General Ira C. Eaker of the United States Army Air Force stepped down from his Dakota at Hendon airport in beleaguered Britain, the war news was as bleak as the February weather. Japanese forces had invaded Singapore, their torpedo planes had sunk two major British battleships, the Americans were making a last stand on Bataan, the Allied armies were retreating across the plains of Libya, the Wehrmacht's Panzer tanks were closing in on Stalingrad, and Atlantic shipping losses to the predatory U-boats were frighteningly high. That very week, the warships *Scharnhorst, Gneisenau,* and *Prinz Eugen* had made a dash through the Channel from their vulnerable anchorages in Brest harbor and had reached the safety of a German port. Desperate attempts by the RAF and the Fleet Air Arm had failed to stop them, and critics of air power wanted to know why; recent operations by RAF bombers, restricted by weather, had been relatively modest. British disciples of aerial bombardment were having a hard time.

Two events, however, held some promise of better days to come: one, Eaker's mission was to prepare the way for the arrival of the U.S. Eighth Air Force; two, the RAF's bomber force had a new commander in the redoubtable Air Chief Marshal Arthur T. Harris who had established his headquarters on the hill above High Wycombe.

The early signs, however, were not encouraging. Eight weeks after Eaker's arrival, the two RAF squadrons then equipped with Avro Lancasters were assigned to attack the

great M.A.N. factory in Augsburg, Bavaria, where the U-boats' diesel engines were being made. The concept of mounting a deep penetration raid in daylight was audacious—as audacious in its way as the attack, hours later, by Colonel Doolittle's carrier-launched force of B-25s on targets in Japan. The thinking at High Wycombe was that the new four-engined bombers, flying at low level in two elements of six, stood a good chance of success, and certainly a better

chance than the lightly armed Wellingtons, underpowered Manchesters, and lumbering Stirlings that formed the bulk of Harris's command, but so much depended on the achievement of surprise. That essential element was lost when, by miscalculation, the first six Lancasters crossed a Luftwaffe fighter field on their passage over France, and four of them were shot down by Me 109s. A fifth was destroyed by flak above the target, as were two of the following element.

Only five aircraft, two of which were badly damaged, struggled back to England on that April evening. John Nettleton, their leader, was awarded the Victoria Cross, Britain's highest military distinction. There was no lack of heroism, and no lack of skill (the factory was struck by thirteen one-thousand-pounders), but there was a fatal lack of firepower. The Lancaster's eight machine guns, firing .303 bullets, had been no match for the cannons of the Me 109s.

It so happened, soon after his arrival, that Eaker had visited Harris's headquarters. The two men had worked together in Washington when Harris led a mission there in 1941, and it was as a friend that the American now sought the Englishman's assistance and advice. Eaker was an advocate of precision bombing, essentially in daylight, by well-armed aircraft flying in tight formation, whereas Harris's usual practice was to send his heavy bombers individually by night, making up for the inevitable loss of accuracy by sheer weight of numbers.

After one or two attempts to persuade the American to "come in with us on the night offensive," and a jocular suggestion that Eaker's reluctance was due to the fact that his airmen could only navigate in daylight, Harris accepted Eaker's point. He postponed the formation of a new RAF bomber group (later to emerge as the Pathfinder Force) to provide the Americans with bases in the Midlands and East Anglia. In addition, the RAF found a fine old building for the Eighth Air Force bomber staff at nearby Daw's Hill Lodge, another for the

Reading maketh a full man; conference a ready man;/ and writing an exact man.

−from *Essays*, by Francis Bacon

If you have tears, prepare to shed them now.

−from *Julius Caesar*, Act III, Sc. 2, by William Shakespeare

We broke out of the undercast and saw the dawn, a great sheet of mother-of-pearl, wrinkled with altocumulus and cirrus, over the continent ahead. Under us, like mud, lay the flat, damp wad of weather that always seemed to cover England and her Channel in those months.

−from *The War Lover*, by John Hersey

left: Air Chief Marshal Arthur T.Harris, right: Brigadier General Ira C.Eaker.

PLAYER'S CIGARETTES

PER NOCTEM VOLAMUS

No. 9 (BOMBER) SQUADRON, R.A.F.

right: An RAF Stirling crew at a Heavy Conversion Unit near Cambridge.

fighter staff at Bushey Hall near Watford and, more importantly, gave the Americans access to a tried and tested nationwide system of communications and control.

An official U.S. record described how the Eighth Air Force was received: "With its Fighter Command guarding the skies by day, the Bomber Command striking the enemy by night, and the Coastal Command sweeping the sea-lanes, the RAF might have taken a condescending attitude towards the advance guard of Americans whose plans were so large and whose means were apparently so small. The RAF took no such attitude. From the start, their generous and sympathetic interest were the keys that unlocked many problems. 'Tell us what you want,' they said. 'If we have it, it is yours.' They might have added, 'Whether or not we need it ourselves.'"

The efficient organization of supplies was crucial to the operation, and it was undertaken by one of Eaker's staff, Major Frederick Castle, whose subsequent career as a combat leader was to add a page of glory to the story of the Eighth; USAAF intelligence officers attended briefings and debriefings at RAF bomber fields; technicians took note of the comments made by British airmen on certain operational shortcomings in the early Flying Fortresses and ordered the appropriate improvements. The Americans were welcomed everywhere they went. At a dinner in his honor, Eaker's speech was short and to the point: "We won't do much talking until we've done more flying. We hope that when we leave, you'll be glad we came. Thank you."

In the azure midafternoon of August 17, 1942, twelve B-17s of the 97th Bomb Group set out from Grafton Underwood on the first Eighth Air Force mission of the war. Taking off at thirty-second intervals, the aircraft climbed up into a sunlit, cloudless sky. Ira Eaker, as commanding general, flew in *Yankee Doodle*, leading the second element of six. The target, appositely, was the railway marshaling yard in Rouen, the city where, five hundred years before, Joan of Arc had died for the liberty of France. Eighteen tons of bombs were dropped from 22,500 feet, and all fell on or near the target. None of the bombers (which the Germans identified as Lancasters) suffered more than superficial damage. Their escort of RAF Spitfires, two of which were lost, destroyed two Messerschmitts and claimed five more as "probables." When the B-17s returned to Grafton Underwood at seven o'clock that evening, the first to land was *Yankee Doodle*, as was right and proper. A message from Harris was brought to Ira Eaker: "Yankee Doodle certainly went to town, and can stick yet another well-earned feather in his cap."

The weather stayed fine, and the 97th flew three more short-range missions with no losses to the bombers. Then, on August 21, nine B-17s en route to Rotterdam were late for the rendezvous with their fighter escort, and the Spitfires, short of fuel, were obliged to leave them halfway to the target. A recall was broadcast later, but for twenty minutes the German fighter pilots had the bombers to themselves. In the ensuing combat, the Fortress gunners claimed to have

4

Recognition views of Messerschmitt Me 109.

destroyed two fighters and to have damaged five, but one straggling bomber, attacked by five FW 190s, was lucky to escape with one man wounded and another dying. It was a salutary engagement.

The Consolidated B-24 Liberators entered the arena on October 9, when the 93rd Bomb Group joined the 97th in an attack on steelworks and locomotive factories in Lille. There were a number of "abortives," with bombs dropped in the Channel, and only 69 of 108 bombers reached the primary target. Nevertheless, it was the heaviest raid yet mounted by the Eighth, a distinction that it would hold, for one reason or another, for the next six months. It was also the first time the bombers had tangled with the Luftwaffe in force. As one navigator put it: "Lille was our first real brawl." In over two hundred combats the enemy fighters only succeeded in shooting down four bombers, but the skill and ferocity demonstrated by the German pilots gave notice of what might be expected in the days to come.

Although enthusiastic claims of over sixty enemy aircraft certainly or probably destroyed were greeted with caution by the debriefing officers and subsequently reduced to forty-two, the figures still showed that the gunners in the well-named Flying Fortresses could give a good account of themselves.

The flak above the target was described by a Liberator crewman as "the worst I've ever seen." The fact that he was flying his first mission detracted a little from the force of the remark, but ensured its remembrance in the annals of the group.

In November 1942, tactics were still in the process of evolving when, seeking greater accuracy, thirty-one B-17s attacked the U-boat pens at St. Nazaire from less than half their normal bombing height. Three aircraft were shot down by flak, and twenty-two were damaged. There were no more medium-altitude attacks by heavy bombers. Then the 305th Bomb Group commander, Colonel Curtis E. LeMay, decided to abandon individual bomb runs: his squadrons would fly in train above the target, and each plane's bombs would be dropped when the leader's load began to fall. Two months later, St. Nazaire was once again the target when LeMay's method was employed. The results were encouraging: more bombs fell near the MPI, the mean point of impact of an ideal strike. Bomb-on-the-leader tactics had been tried and proven.

When Ray Wild arrived at Podington to join the 92nd Bomb Group, one of his first actions was to look up an RAF pilot who had been a classmate during training in the States. "He and I went out," said Wild, "and had a couple of beers with some of his buddies. They felt that we Americans were out of our minds. They had tried daylight bombing and it just wasn't feasible. They said we'd get the hell shot out of us. They were right: on the first few raids we did get the hell shot out of us. But those Limeys did something that sure would scare me—night bombing. They'd come in over a target a minute apart, one guy this way, another guy from another point in the compass. This would scare me to death. They had tremendous intestinal fortitude.

They were also realistic in that they couldn't bomb by daylight. Those Lancs were built to carry bombs, and not to protect themselves, while we could. So long as we stayed in tight formation, we could throw a lot of lead out in the right direction at the right time."

By the time spring came to England in 1943, several lessons had been learned, most of them the hard way. By now, every Eighth Air Force crewman knew that, to the Luftwaffe, the sight of a crippled airplane or a straggler was like the taste of blood to a school of piranha. On future missions, the bombers would fly in combat box formations of lead, high, and low squadrons, planned to provide the maximum defensive firepower. At the IP (initial point), some miles from the target, the squadrons would move into line astern, bomb with the lead planes, and reform at a rally point for the homeward flight.

Mechanics tend the 97BG B-17E *Yankee Doodle* at Grafton Underwood in the summer of 1942. In this aircraft Brigadier General Ira Eaker led the second element of B-17s attacking the Rouen marshaling yards on August 17, 1942.

below: An RAF Whitley being readied for a raid in 1942, right: Sewing parachutes for the RAF, below right: Maintaining the Merlin engines of an Avro Lancaster bomber in 1942. The sturdy and reliable Lanc was the first heavy bomber able to carry huge quantities of high explosives over great distances. It was the workhorse of RAF Bomber Command in the bombing offensive against Germany.

When after many battles past,/ Both tir'd with blows, make peace at last, What is it, after all, the people get?/ Why! taxes, widows, wooden legs, and debt.

—from *Almanack*, by Francis Moore

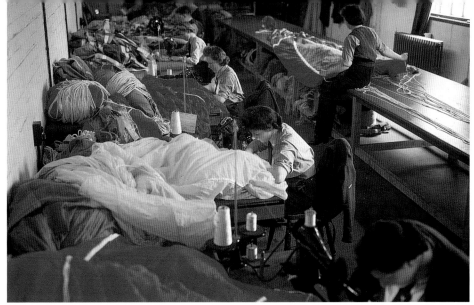

The feeble tremble before opinion, the foolish defy it,/ the wise judge it, the skillful direct it.

—Mme. Jeanne Roland

England expects every man to do his duty.

—Admiral Lord Nelson

Unusual techniques in construction were part of what made the Vickers Wellington, below, and the DeHavilland Mosquito, right, special. The Mosquito was too fast to be intercepted on bombing missions. Only the fighter variants carried guns.

Both the Allied bomber force commanders now had a number of twin-engine planes at their disposal. The Eighth had formed a group of B-26 Martin Marauders, and would soon form more, while the RAF Bomber Command was being reinforced by squadrons of de Havilland Mosquitoes. The heavily armed, six-man-crew Marauders, flying in two boxes of eighteen airplanes each, would attack the industrial targets in France and the Low Countries with one-ton loads of bombs; the versatile Mosquitoes, crewed by a pilot and a navigator, unarmed but flying higher and faster than any twin piston-engine aircraft yet conceived, were being increasingly used as pathfinders by the RAF, and by the Eighth for photo reconnaissance; as Harris's "Light Night Striking Force" they would eventually carry two-ton "cookies" to Berlin on four nights out of six.

Eaker and Harris were agreed: between them they would wield a rapier by day and a bludgeon by night, and 1943 would be a big year for the bombers.

I am a man of peace, God knows how I love peace;/ but I hope I shall never be such a coward as to mistake oppression for peace.

—Louis Kossuth

Cheer up, the worst is yet to come.

—Philander Johnson

"THE ENEMY must be attacked by day and by night," announced Sir Archibald Sinclair, the British Air Secretary, "so that he may have no respite from the Allied blows, so that his defensive resources may be taxed to the utmost limit. But day and night bombing are separate though complementary tasks. Each requires a strategic plan, a tactical execution and a supporting organization adapted to its special needs. So there has been a division of labor. To one force—the Eighth Bomber Command—has been allotted the task of day bombing. To the other force—our Bomber Command—the task of night bombing. The methods are different, but the aim is the same: to paralyze the armed forces of Germany by disrupting the war economy by which they are sustained."

The civil servant who prepared those phrases for his minister had no need to pull his punches. In the year just passed, bombing policy had changed. The RAF's attacks were no longer restricted to "military targets," and gone were the days when only propaganda leaflets could be dropped on cities. The early German air attacks on Warsaw, Rotterdam, Coventry, and London had shown what could be done, and Britain's mood had hardened. "They have sown the wind," said Air Chief Marshal Harris, "now they will reap the whirlwind."

Initially, there had been little difference in the way the bomber tactics of the Luftwaffe and the RAF evolved. Both had begun with daylight raids—the Germans on what then had seemed a massive scale—both had suffered heavy losses from the other's air de-

13

ALLIES

We are coming, Father Abraham, three hundred thousand more.

–J. S. Gibbons

Somebody said that it couldn't be done, / But he with a chuckle replied / That "maybe" it couldn't, but he would be one / Who wouldn't say so till he'd tried./ So he buckled right in with the trace of a grin on his face. If he worried he hid it. / He started to sing as he tackled the thing That couldn't be done, and he did it.

–from *Tee Emm*

Here is a toast that I want to give/ To a fellow I'll never know:/ To the fellow who's going to take my place/ When it's time for me to go.

–"To My Successor," by Louis E. Thayer

below: Prime Minister Winston Churchill poses with a Tommy gun in 1940, right: The crew of *Buckeye Belle,* a 384BG B-17G at Grafton Underwood.

fenses, and both had been obliged to seek the cover of the night. It was in the way the opposing forces developed and conducted their night operations that the differences emerged. A major factor was that the German aircraft industry was never able to provide the Luftwaffe with an effective heavy bomber, whereas the British airplane designers, responding to the RAF's requirement, produced the huge four-engined Short Stirling, the Handley/Page Halifax, and, at last, the Avro Lancaster. Then, to find their targets, the German crews depended on visual checkpoints such as estuaries and rivers, or, when bombing through the overcast, by flying along a radio beam transmitted from Europe; the RAF, meanwhile, was developing radar navigation and all-weather methods of pyrotechnic target-marking.

The main contrast, however, between the two offensives was in their weight and scale. While the Eighth's day offensive was gathering momentum, and Harris's new heavies flew in growing numbers to pound industrial targets deep inside the Reich, the German raids dwindled until they could be regarded, strategically at least, as of nuisance value only. Although Hitler still had some lethal shots left in his locker—the "little blitz" on London in early 1944, and the "doodlebugs" and rockets that prolonged Britain's ordeal until their launching sites were smashed—from that time on, German factories were trundling out fighters, not bombers, and that was no way to win a war. There can be no doubt that the enemy was forced into this defensive posture by the USAAF's daylight raids.

For the participants—the men who flew the airplanes—there were many differences between a day mission in a Fortress or a Liberator and a night operation in a British bomber. For one thing, the RAF crews tried not to tangle with the night fighters, and used various tactics—electronic countermeasures, spoof attacks, and feints—to put them off the scent. The fliers of the Eighth, on the other hand, deliberately set out to take the fighters on: with the great formations shining in the sunlight and leaving condensation trails for many miles behind them, they presented a challenge no defending air force could refuse. In this, the USAAF's air divisions could be likened to regiments of cavalry, riding high upon a hillside, silhouetted on the skyline, with guidons fluttering and bugles blowing the charge; "Butch" Harris's men, on the other hand, were more like the infantry, moving through the lines in darkness, with blackened faces and muffled tread.

It was when they reached their targets that the Allied fliers shared a mutual experience. There the reception was very much the same; it just looked rather different. The crewmen saw ahead of them an apparently impenetrable barrier of flak, standing in their way from the start of the bomb run to the release point and beyond. At night it appeared as a million sparks among the groping searchlights; by day, as a sky full of lumps of dirty cotton. That was what they had to fly through, day or night. There was no point in trying to dodge between the shell bursts: in evading one they might fly into

right: Betty's bar in York was popular with Allied airmen during the war, center: The High Street, Lavenham in 1944, below: The tower at Tholthorpe, where RCAF crews flew their operational missions in Halifaxes.

left: Surviving GI wall art in Lavenham hut, home to the 487BG, below: Lead and low squadrons of the 487BG cross the Brittany peninsula en route to attack a target at Royan, France, on April 15, 1945.

The English nation is never so great as in adversity.

—Benjamin Disraeli

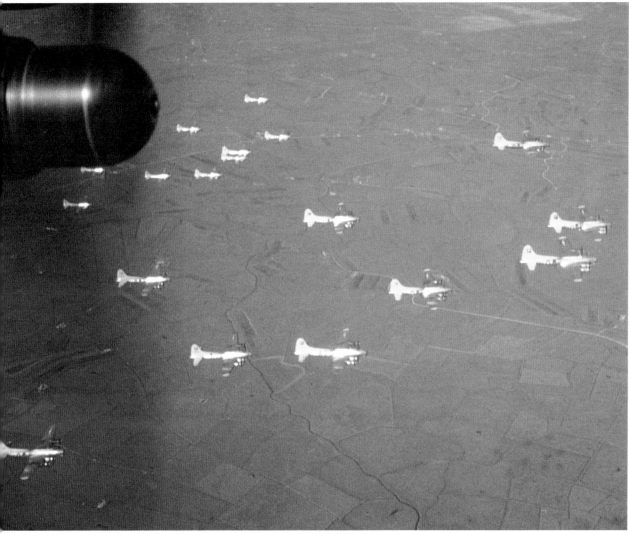

another. Nor was there any chance of dodg-
ing, even if they wanted to, once the airplane
was committed to the bomb run. From that
moment on, it was the man with his thumb
on the bomb-release button who was in control, and he had eyes only for the aiming
point or the lead plane's bomb bay.

However similar the physical experiences over the target, there was a marked

distinction in the human aspect. The crewmen of a USAAF bomber were flying close to
guys they knew: at the controls of the Fortress above their starboard wing was the
pilot's buddy; one of the navigator's poker
school was flying in the nose of the airplane
on their left; the gunners in the lead ship
shared a billet with their own. When any of
those aircraft lost a battle with a fighter, or a

flak battery scored a lethal hit, there was a personal interest in seeing who got out. Everyone should, of course, be concentrating on his job, but when you knew that Ed was in that ship, and little Virgil from Ohio, you couldn't help but watch and whisper, "Come on, you guys, get the hell out of there!"

At night it was different, and utterly impersonal. No one could identify the men who had just disappeared in a blinding flash of light; no one had a clue who was trapped inside that burning Lancaster making a meteoric arc across the sky. The crew of a night bomber were seven men essentially alone.

There is no part of the eight thousand square miles of England known as East Anglia that stands over four hundred feet above the sea. This, and the fact that the land is agricultural, containing no more than a half-dozen towns of any size, made it eminently suitable for siting bomber airfields. Some had been constructed before the war began and, by the end of 1944, a total of ninety-eight, RAF or USAAF, were operational. If you walked ten miles in any direction from, say, Rattlesden or Deopham Green, you would be within hailing distance of another bomber base.

Further north in Lincolnshire the scene was much the same. Twenty-five RAF bases lay between the coastline and the river Trent, and from 10,000 feet on a clear night over Lincoln, you could see the Drem lights of a dozen fields. Some were so close that their traffic patterns overlapped; at Scamp-

ton, for example, when a southwest wind prevailed, the pilots would fly a right-hand pattern, while their neighbors at Dunholme Lodge made their circuits to the left. For both bomber forces, climbing to altitude, whether in darkness or in cloud by day, was a hazardous procedure, and midair collisions inevitably occurred. Every British pilot breathed a sigh of relief when he turned on his first course, every American when he emerged into the clear.

In press releases, the RAF seldom publicized the altitudes at which its bombers flew. The USAAF, with no cause for secrecy, revealed that the Fortresses could operate at 30,000 feet. The information intrigued the British public: how did the crews survive at such a height? Perhaps, it was argued, the well-established fact that Americans were fed from early childhood on T-bone steaks and pumpkin pie contributed to their extraordinary stamina. In the interests of medical research, an English doctor accompanied a Fortress crew on a training exercise. That he became unconscious halfway through the flight merely reinforced the theory that the Yanks were supermen.

The Eighth's combat formations were planned with two main purposes in mind: one, to maximize the firepower of the bombers' guns, and two, to concentrate the bombing pattern on the MPI while ensuring that no bombs hit another aircraft as they fell. These were considerations that had little application to the RAF's night bombers, in which the crews found their own way to the target, fought individual battles with the

The time will come, when thou shalt lift thine eyes / To watch a long-drawn battle in the skies, / While aged peasants, too amazed for words, / Stare at the flying fleets of wond'rous birds. / England, so long mistress of the sea, / Where winds and waves confess her sovereignty, / Her ancient triumphs yet on high shall bear, / And reign, the sovereign of the conquered air.

—translated from Thomas Gray's "Luna Habitabilis," Cambridge, 1797

Oh, God! that bread
should be so dear,/ and
flesh and blood so
cheap!

—from "Song of a Shirt,"
by Thomas Hood

top: A runway-in-use
marker at the derelict
control tower, RAF
Wymeswold.

left: The Woodman Inn, a pub set on the verge of Nuthampstead airfield, WWII home of the 398BG, right: A pub sign at The Flying Fortress, located on the northern side of the former 94BG base, Rougham, a few miles east of Bury St.Edmunds, below: A Nissen hut at Rougham in 1988.

fighters (but only if they had to), and made the bomb runs on their own. The operations staff at High Wycombe did their best to limit "friendly" damage by splitting the attacks into waves, each lasting ten or fifteen minutes, but the inevitable navigation errors meant that some Halifaxes and Stirlings infringed the timing of the higher-flying Lancasters, and vice versa. Many British aircraft were found, on return, to have been damaged by bombs from aircraft flying above them, and no one will ever know how many more went down. Aiming point photographs, brought home by Lancasters, often showed the black silhouettes of four-engined aircraft that had flown into the cross wires as the bombs began to fall.

Although the organization and structure of command in the USAAF and the RAF were basically similar, there were certain differences in style and designations. Commissioned officers in the U.S. Army Air Force naturally held military ranks, while the RAF, on gaining the status of an independent service toward the end of World War I, had adopted new ones of its own. In ascending order, an American second lieutenant ranked with a British pilot officer, a first lieutenant with a flying officer, a captain with a flight lieutenant, a major with a squadron leader, a lieutenant colonel with a wing commander, a colonel with a group captain, a brigadier general with an air commodore and so on.

The basic combat unit in both forces was the squadron, and one or two RAF bomber squadrons occupied a "station"; a number of stations were controlled by group HQ, sometimes with a "base station" as an intermediary, and the group staffs answered to the commander in chief at High Wycombe. Although the RAF fighter squadrons might form wings for combat purposes, in the bomber force the wing was no longer an operational formation. In the Eighth Air Force, groups of four squadrons occupied a "base," fifteen groups comprised a bombardment wing (later to be known as an air division), which responded to the commanding general, Eighth Bomber Command Headquarters at Daws Hill.

The problems of nomenclature occasioned by the fact that "groups" and "wings" meant different things to the USAAF and the RAF, and that the RAF did not recognize an "air division," were compounded by the anomalies of rank. In the prewar RAF, these had borne some relation to the holder's duties: pilot officers were pilots, flying officers flew airplanes, flight lieutenants led flights, and squadron leaders led squadrons. The war had brought upgradings: the command of main force flights and squadrons rated one rank more, and two more in No. 8 Group, the Pathfinder Force. The USAAF, on the other hand, saw no need to escalate its gradings. The American commander of a Fortress squadron, visiting his equivalent on a British pathfinder base, might have been surprised to find himself heavily outranked. It may have been as well for interservice harmony that these visits were infrequent: squadron commanders, RAF or USAAF, had little time for making social calls.

Man is not the creature of circumstances, Circumstances are the creatures of men.

—from *Vivian Grey*, by Benjamin Disraeli

They go from strength to strength.

—Psalms 84:7.

No army can withstand the strength of an idea whose time has come.

—Victor Hugo

The crew of "H Harry" have tea at a wagon that was given to the RAF by the American YMCA. Canadian YMCA workers talk with the men near their Halifax bomber. The crew has just returned from the thousand-bomber raid of May 30-31, 1943, on Cologne.

GETTING UP FOR A MISSION

And please'd th' Almighty's orders to perform. Rides in the whirlwind and directs the storm.

—from *The Campaign*, by Joseph Addison

War is the science of destruction.

—John S. C. Abbott

Mason And Dixon, a B-17G of the 100BG, at Thorpe Abbotts.

EVERYONE AT SOME TIME has awakened in the morning knowing that a big day lies ahead. It might be a crucial business meeting, an opening night onstage, your first match with the "A" team, a university examination. You know it has to happen, and in a way you're glad of it; in another way you dread it, and you wish it were tomorrow, not today. All bomber crewmen experienced such feelings, and with some intensity. They woke to many big days, and knew that any one might be their last on earth.

The start of one such big day for a combat flier was described by ball turret gunner Ken Stone of the 381st Bomb Group: "The night officer came around every barracks and woke us up. As a gunner, you had no prior notification. If a mission was called, they just came and woke you up. If they said to hurry, we usually didn't shave. That kind of irritated when you had your oxygen mask on, but I didn't have much of a beard then, anyway. They gave us time to have breakfast. I'd have eggs—real eggs—fried or scrambled, and lots of Spam. I swore I'd never eat Spam again. But it was regular food, the same as the officers ate."

The reveille routine at Debach in the time of Larry Bird, who flew twenty-three missions with the 493rd Bomb Group, was rather better organized. "You'd go to the bulletin board at five or six o'clock in the afternoon to check which crews were flying next day. If you were down to fly, you'd try and get to bed a little earlier than usual."

Paul Sink, the rear gunner in Bird's crew, took that sequence further: "After

24

BRIEFING ROOM.
ADMITTANCE BY PASS ONLY.

FARLOOSE GOOSE

above: Entering a mission briefing on an 8AF base.

Youth! youth! how buoyant are the hopes; they turn like marigolds, toward the sunny side.

—from "The Four Bridges," by Jean Ingelow

far left: USAAF aircrew have just learned that their target for today (March 6, 1944) is to be Berlin, above right: 8AF aircrew ride out to their aircraft at a Midlands bomber station.
above: Breakfast with enlisted men at Grafton Underwood, the 384BG base, left: 1st Lt. V.A.McCarty aboard a large bomb at his Flixton (Bungay) base in 1944.

breakfast, we went to the main briefing. The room was dimly lit like a theater, with huge maps on the wall. A jagged line showed the courses, the initial point, the bomb run, and the rally point. It showed where you would pick up the fighter cover, where you would lose it, and where you would pick it up again."

"After the main briefing," Bird continued, "the pilots, navigators, and bombardiers had individual briefings, while the rest of the crew collected their guns from the armament shack. We went out to the hardstands, got the props pulled through and the guns installed, and gave the airplane a complete preflight check—intercom and oxygen systems and everything. By then it was usually getting to be almost daylight. Sometimes the moon would still be visible. The pilots got the engines ticking over, and we'd all move out and go down the taxi strip in a long line. Then we'd wait our turn to take off. It would be getting lighter all the time."

Charles J. Bosshardt, who flew twenty missions in a B-24 of the 458th Bomb Group, recalled one of those navigators' briefings at Horsham St. Faith in February 1945. "That morning, they got us up at three-thirty and we were briefed for the marshaling yards at Rheine. We navigators were always in there at briefing long after the rest of the crews had gone out to the aircraft, and I was usually in a sweat when I joined them. This time, I was the last one out. I piled my equipment into a truck and set out to find the plane. We drove out past all the 753rd Squadron revetments but I couldn't spot it. I

28

far left: A 93BG gunner exits a Hardwick crew room, left: *Rugged But Right,* a 493BG B-24 Liberator, below: A 100BG B-17G, *Humpty Dumpty.*

"It was really a very simple, adventurous, and exciting time."

David Parry, pilot, 390BG

left: RAF bomber crew are briefed for a raid, right: Dressing and pre-flight preparations in a locker room of 467 Squadron at RAF Waddington, a few miles south of Lincoln, below: An RAF Halifax being attended in Yorkshire.

had the driver turn around. I jumped out and checked a few that looked like U141 but none of them was it. In desperation I asked another pilot to check his flimsy for the revetment number. He told me that my plane was not in this revetment. I was getting worried by then because it was just a few minutes until stations time. Finally I started checking the marshaled ships. The first few were from another squadron, then came our squadron. The third one up was U141. I ran up and got our nose gunner to go back to the truck with me and help carry my junk. We trotted back and got it and started weaving our way through the prop blades. Just as I dumped my stuff in the nose the pilot started warming the engines. I dragged my body up on the flight deck and waited for takeoff. I was soaked in perspiration."

"As a lead crew," said radar operator Sidney Rapoport of the 94th Bomb Group, "we knew about the mission before the other crews and we were woken earlier. That was an interesting experience, getting up at two in the morning in a black winter night in East Anglia. It was icy outside when you went to the latrine. It was important to shave, and looking in the mirror, I always used to think: 'Mirror, mirror, is this the last time I'm going to look into you?'"

The RAF crews' preparation for a night operation varied little from one station to another. Jack Clift of 463 Squadron described the beginning of a normal day. "I would go down to the flight engineers' office, the pilots to theirs, the navigators to theirs, and so on. The section leaders would tell us if there was

anything new we ought to know about. By lunchtime, we'd have found out if ops were on, and later they'd put the battle order up showing which crews were scheduled. If we were on the list, we'd take the aircraft for a test flight, just to make sure everything was okay. About teatime, you'd know what the petrol load was, and that would give you some idea about the trip. If it was 2,154 gallons—maximum petrol—you knew it was a long one. Most of ours were 2154s. There would be separate briefings for us and the other crew members, and then the main briefing, with the CO and the wing commander. When you walked in, you looked at the big map on the wall and the red ribbon zigzagging out to the target—we never went straight there—and you'd say, 'Bloody hell, another snorter.'"

Although RAF briefings usually took place some twelve hours after the USAAF's, they were very similar in content and in sequence. They would include a description of the target and its strategic significance, the intended tactics, the system of control, the heights and courses to be flown, the expected opposition, the assigned supporting forces, and a weather forecast. There would be a time check for the navigators and some words of exhortation from the colonel or group captain in command. On a USAAF base, at this point, it was not uncommon for the chaplain to offer a short prayer. RAF crews were given no such overt benison before they took to the air, nor would the padre normally be present; he was available, however, for those who sought his blessing,

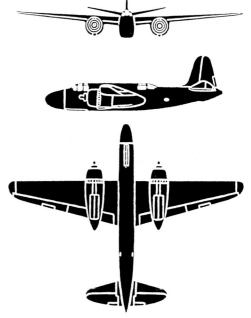

Dinghy said to me, "Can I have your egg if you don't come back?" This was the well-known corney joke because each crew was allowed to have an egg after a successful operational mission, and eggs were considered delicacies because they were very scarce. I said, "Sugar off," and told him to do something very difficult to himself.

—from *Enemy Coast Ahead*, by Guy Gibson

Recognition views of Douglas DB-7 Boston.

The hole and the patch should be commensurate.

—from a 1787 letter by Thomas Jefferson

and would probably be waiting when the crews returned, dispensing mugs of cocoa and a word of greeting before they were de-briefed.

"After the briefing," Jack Clift continued, "there'd be a meal, a nice meal of bacon and eggs, and then you'd relax, lie down on your bed, and have a rest for half an hour. Of course, you'd keep thinking about what you were going to be doing for the next ten hours or so. And then, down to the crew room, pick up the parachutes, get dressed in your gear, into the crew bus, out to the flights, into the aircraft, and away."

Clift had the advantage of being based at Waddington, a compact, prewar station; facilities on other fields were more widely spread out. Once an airman left his billet in the morning, he had left it for the day, as Reg Payne of 50 Squadron remembered of his time at Skellingthorpe. "If there was a break between the flying meal and takeoff, we never went back to the billet, because it was a mile and a half away from the mess, and the mess was a mile from the operations room. We just used to sit down somewhere and close our eyes for a while."

Briefings at Skellingthorpe, as Payne recalled them, demanded more than average attention. "The CO was very strict. He'd brief you on what time start-up and takeoff were, what time the first wave set off, the course, the engine revs and boost, the height you had to be at the first turning point, what colors the markers were . . . and then he would call someone out, any crew member, and make him repeat it in front of everybody. If

Be still sad heart, and cease repining;/ Behind the clouds is the sun still shining;/ Thy fate is the common fate of all, Into each life some rain must fall,/ Some days must be dark and dreary.

—from "The Rainy Day," by Henry Wadsworth Longfellow.

above: Reg Payne of 50 Squadron , based at Skellingthorpe in WWII, above right: cookhouse art at the Shipdham base of the 44BG, right: A retired Morris Minor in a wartime shelter at Lavenham, Suffolk.

you made a cockup of it, and he thought you hadn't been listening, you were struck off the raid, and a substitute would fly in your place. That was considered a black mark for the crew. I was a wireless op, and a lot of it didn't mean much to me, but I used to memorize it all."

The body clock of the average young man tells him to be active in the daytime and to sleep at night; it does not readily accept a different regime. To help the night bomber men in staying alert throughout their missions, the medicos supplied caffeine-based stimulants known as "wakey-wakey" pills. "We'd never take them," said Payne, "until the aircraft was rumbling down the runway, because we'd had many occasions when the raid was scrubbed at the last minute and we'd be up the creek—awake all night for nothing."

Let us have faith that right makes might, and in that faith let us, to the end, dare to do our duty as we understand it.

—Abraham Lincoln.

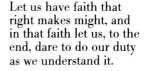

above left: Remains of a Tannoy loudspeaker at Deenethorpe, home of the 401BG, above: Jack Clift was a Lancaster flight engineer at RAF Waddington, left: A bit of bomb bay door found at the crash site of a 487BG B-24 near Lavenham.

Heavy bomb damage
in the city of Cologne.

WHEN FRANKLIN DELANO ROOSEVELT, Winston Churchill, and Joseph Stalin conferred at Casablanca in January 1943, the fate of two commands—Eaker's and Harris's—rested in their hands. If they accepted Stalin's demand for a second front in Europe (and Roosevelt was sympathetic to the Russian argument), *Overlord* would be mounted, and the strategic air offensive would be finished before it had properly begun. General Eisenhower would take charge as the Supreme Commander Allied Forces Europe, and the bombers would be totally committed to ground-support operations. It would thus be good-bye to the bomber chiefs' dream of reducing Germany's morale and matériel to the point where the Allied armies would merely be required as an occupation force.

Even if the British view prevailed—that the *Overlord* invasion should wait upon *Husky* (an advance into Europe through Sicily and Italy)—the bomber commanders still had problems in their own backyards. The admirals, both in Washington and London, were propounding that the airplanes under construction for the Eighth Air Force should go to the Pacific, that Harris's bombers should concentrate on U-boats, and that the H2S radars his navigators sorely needed should instead be fitted in antisubmarine patrol planes of Coastal Command.

Another, if lesser, problem was that not everyone in Britain supported Harris's campaign. Quoting the devastation of Essen and Cologne as instances, a prominent churchman was leading a number of gentle souls in protesting against what they saw as a slaughter of the innocent, and two respected, albeit armchair, strategists were complaining that an undue proportion of the national war effort was being absorbed by Harris's command. The great majority, however, of the British people remained solidly in favor of the bomber offensive. Most seemed to understand that Queensberry rules and padded gloves were out when you were fighting for your life. Harris's aircrews stood high in the public's affection and esteem, perhaps not quite so high as the fighter pilots had while the Battle of Britain was being fought above their homes, but high enough to ensure the bomber boys a welcome when they spent an evening in the "local" or a leave in town.

As things turned out, Winston Churchill was well satisfied with the outcome of the summit conference. However readily he had welcomed Russia as an ally, he was not altogether displeased that the Wehrmacht and the Red Army should have another year in which to grind each other down. Eaker and Harris, too, came out of Casablanca pretty well. The essence of the Moroccan deliberations, as distilled and decanted by the planning staffs, eventually reached the bomber chiefs as the *Pointblank* directive. "Your primary aim," it began, "will be the progressive destruction and dislocation of the German military, industrial and economic system, and the undermining of the morale of the German people to a point where their capacity for armed resistance is fatally weakened."

It says much for Eaker's staff work and his powers of persuasion that, although none

Nothing begins and nothing ends,/ That is not paid for with moan;/ For we are born in others' pain,/ And perish in our own.

—from "Daisy," by Francis Thompson

"Merseburg was the most difficult target in WWII, and it's never mentioned. This was the one that sent shivers down your spine when you went in for the briefing and saw this long red tape across the English Channel and deep into Germany."

Sidney Rapoport, radar bombardier, 94BG

If an injury has to be done to a man it should be so severe that his vengeance need not be feared.

—from *The Prince*, by Machiavelli

left: At Pinetree, High Wycombe, an 8AF lead navigator plots a mission course through known flak concentrations, right: Personnel at Pinetree examine a teleprinter tape of mission specifications being sent to the heavy bomb groups, below: the results of an 8AF raid on the Krupps gun works at Essen.

of his bombers had yet flown over Germany and half his sorties had failed to reach their targets, his imprint was heavy on what followed in the document. Far from requiring him to renounce daylight bombing and join the night offensive, as the British had suggested, the directive authorized continued day attacks "to destroy objectives unsuitable for night bombing, to sustain pressure on German morale, to impose heavy losses on the German day fighter force, and to contain its strength away from the Russian and Mediterranean theaters."

There was a sop for the admirals in that the first objectives on the *Pointblank* list were U-boat facilities; airfields and airplane factories came next; and then, in order, ball-bearing plants, oil refineries, synthetic rubber works, and transportation targets. It also transpired that an Eaker reference to bombing "round the clock" had found favor with the British prime minister, who had rolled the phrase around his tongue in Morocco and used it ever after as his own.

None of this was any skin off Harris's nose. "When precision targets are bombed by the Eighth Air Force in daylight," he read with satisfaction in the follow-up to the directive, "the effort should be completed and complemented by RAF attacks against the surrounding industrial area at night." "This," he later wrote, "gave me a very wide range of choice and allowed me to attack pretty well any German industrial city of 100,000 inhabitants and above." So, for the citizens of Essen and Cologne, *Pointblank* meant that the worst was yet to come; for the

people of Hamburg, Frankfurt, Stuttgart, Mannheim, and all points east, that the bombers would get to them in turn; for the Berliners, that the time was not far off when they would be subjected to the greatest air onslaught ever to be mounted on a European city.

Very few RAF men had any doubt that they were doing what they had to do. For them, the problem wasn't one of ethics but of method—of technique. Many of the pilots, trained to high standards in formation flying, regretted they never had the chance to use that skill; when they watched the air armadas of the Eighth go forth to war, there was a certain envy in their gaze; the bomb-aimers, too, often wished that they were equipped with the USAAF's apparatus—the computerized, gyrostabilized Norden Mark XV bombsight—with which, claimed the bombardiers (after a drink or two), they could drop a five-hundred-pounder into a pickle barrel from 25,000 feet; many an air gunner would have willingly exchanged all his .303 machine guns for one American .50-caliber.

One major problem the bomber forces shared was the European weather. At an early meeting, Harris had warned Eaker (perhaps with some exaggeration) that on four days out of five his bombardiers would never see the ground. "So we'll bring the bombs home and try another day," had been the American's reply, but as time went on, Eaker realized that his crews were flying too many noneffective missions. In cloudy conditions Eaker and General Anderson (the

above: Fred Allen was a Lissett-based Halifax rear gunner. His aircraft was called *Friday the Thirteenth*.

Watchman, what of the night?

—Isaiah 21:11.

Morality is a private and costly luxury.

—from *The Education of Henry Adams*, by Henry B. Adams

The people are the city.

—from *Coriolanus*, Act III, Sc. 1, by William Shakespeare

The Germans had the whole vast industrial capacity of the Continent at their disposal, and even if by a miracle we had been able to destroy all worthwhile ball-bearing plants at a time when we were finding it difficult to identify and hit much larger targets, this would only have embarrassed, not stopped, the German war effort. Yet I was actually told that I should be justified in accepting such losses to achieve the destruction of Schweinfurt as would put the whole of the bomber force out of action for two months. The target experts paid no attention to the fact that Schweinfurt was too small and distant a town for us to be able to find and hit in 1943.

From *Bomber Offensive* by Sir Arthur Harris

Operationally, the idea of area bombing was to attack an aiming point which lay at the centre of a large area whose destruction would be useful. It was, in other words, a method of making bombs which missed the aiming point contribute to the destruction of the German war machine. Since nearly all bombs were missing the aiming point, there was a certain logic about the idea.

—from *The Bombing Offensive Against Germany*, by Noble Frankland

Eighth's bomber chief) were obliged to turn, as Harris had before them, to the magic eye of radar ("Mickey" to the Eighth), aided when required by target-marking pyrotechnics. This was a method to which the RAF was well accustomed, and for the purposes of saturation bombing it was adequate. For precision bombing it was not, but that had to be accepted. The round-the-clock policy required sustained attack, and in much of Europe's winter (and often in summer) you either bombed through cloud or not at all.

To achieve concentration or accuracy using ground target markers was difficult enough; using sky markers over thick cloud cover, it was practically impossible. Then, the parachuted flares marked a point in the sky through which the bombs should fall. Theoretically, if the aircraft's speed and heading were both exactly right, they should go on to hit the target: realistically, they could miss it by many a mile. Certainly, the results could not compare with those to be achieved by the human eyeball looking down through a bombsight—and especially through the Norden.

It was only on the nights when the sky was clear and moonlit, or at times when a feature of the target—a river or a coastline—showed up clearly in the light of flares and fires, that the RAF crews made the sort of bomb runs for which they had been trained. For the most part they depended on the target-marking efforts of No. 8 Group, the specially selected elite Pathfinder Force flying Lancasters, Halifaxes, and Mosquitoes, using the latest types of radar, and led by the bril-

liant, if independently minded, Australian Air Vice-Marshal D.C.T. Bennett.

"Donald Bennett," said Lancaster pilot Alan Forman, "was a highly qualified man, and he would tolerate no backsliding at all. None whatsoever. He often came around the squadrons and he complained about creep-back. What happened was a bomb-aimer would be keen to get rid of his bombs and he'd bomb a little short of the aiming point. The next aircraft would be shorter, and so on, shorter and shorter. Creep-back. That's why the PFF was formed. They kept re-marking the actual aiming point. They used colored markers, and the Germans got on to this. They used markers on the ground to distract the bombers. The PFF had to keep changing the colors. The master bomber would say, 'Bomb on the greens. Ignore the yellows in the northeast corner.' "

Keith Newhouse, who had flown his B-24, *Wallowing Wilbur*, from Florida via Trinidad, Brazil, and French Morocco to join the Eighth Air Force, was to fly thirty-three missions with the 467th Bomb Group, and to earn the DFC and Air Medal with three clusters. He made this diary note a few days after his arrival at Rackheath field in Norfolk: "Wednesday, March 22, 1944. I spent an hour or two in our war room. All the dope the Eighth has on prospective targets is consolidated there for the study of combat crew officers. Maps, photographs and pertinent data. Heavy flak concentrations are marked clearly, and anything that will help to identify the targets is brought to one's attention."

On the big daylight missions, however,

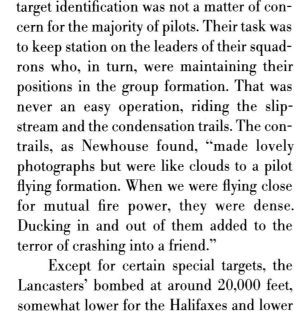

target identification was not a matter of concern for the majority of pilots. Their task was to keep station on the leaders of their squadrons who, in turn, were maintaining their positions in the group formation. That was never an easy operation, riding the slipstream and the condensation trails. The contrails, as Newhouse found, "made lovely photographs but were like clouds to a pilot flying formation. When we were flying close for mutual fire power, they were dense. Ducking in and out of them added to the terror of crashing into a friend."

Except for certain special targets, the Lancasters' bombed at around 20,000 feet, somewhat lower for the Halifaxes and lower still for the Stirlings and Wellingtons. The B-24 formations of the Eighth sought to make their bomb runs at heights between 20,000 and 23,000 feet, while the B-17s generally occupied the height-band from 24,000 to 27,000. Occasionally the weather required them to climb higher, as Paul Sink recalled: "It was when we went to Bitterfeld on March 17, 1945. At 30,000 feet we were just above the cloud. All the guns on the airplane were frozen solid, and the German fighters had the same problem. The strangest thing was that I saw a parachute floating down from above us, on the left side of our airplane. The temperature then was probably sixty degrees below, and there was this parachute with a person hanging from it."

Throughout the latter part of the air offensive, the enemy oil industry always had a high priority on the USAAF's target list, but it seldom featured on the RAF's. This

was understandable: apart from the fact that Arthur Harris was suspicious of what he called "panacea" targets, oil installations, with their compact layout, were not entirely suitable for area attack. In June 1944, when four attacks were made on oil plants in the Ruhr, the results were disappointing and the losses were severe. Some eight hundred sorties cost over ninety aircraft. An attack three months later, on Sterkrade and Bottrop, was no more successful: only twenty-five bomb-aimers out of nearly three hundred claimed to have found the target through the cloud; the rest dropped their loads on "the estimated positions of other Ruhr cities."

That operation stayed in the memory of Fred Allen, rear gunner of Halifax *Friday the Thirteenth*, based at Lissett near the Yorkshire coast, for an instance of what he described as "finger trouble." "The first time round," said Allen, "the bomb-aimer forgot to fuse the bombs. Next attempt, he didn't open the bomb doors. When you didn't bomb, you had to turn to port and go around again. Everybody else was turning starboard. The Jerries weren't much concerned with the ones that had bombed, but they were with those that hadn't. It got a bit hot. The skipper said, 'If you don't drop the buggers this time, I will'—meaning he'd use the jettison bar. We dropped them, all right."

"We'd generally have three targets," said Lawrence Drew, who flew a B-17 with the 384th Bomb Group throughout the last five months of war. "A primary, a secondary, and a tertiary. Well, a lot of times the leader couldn't hit the primary, so he'd go on to the

secondary, then if you couldn't hit any of the three we'd have some targets of opportunity. You'd search around for anywhere you thought would do some good. You couldn't hang around too long because you'd be back too late and get into a conflict with the timing of the RAF."

41

TAKEOFF AND ASSEMBLY

50656 A.C

above: B-17s are being fuelled at Ridgewell, center: Remains of a runway light at RAF Langar, bottom: The store for parachutes at RAF Bottesford.

ON THE BOMBER STATIONS of the Eighth, the ground crews have filled the gas tanks overnight, checked the engines, and serviced all the systems. The armorers are still winching five-hundred-pounders into the bomb bay when the first crewmen arrive in the early-morning hours. The gunners install their weapons in the turrets, the radio operator tests the RT and the intercom, and the top gunner, doubling as engineer, checks the oxygen supply and generally prepares the airplane for flight. The next truck to come by brings the pilots, the navigator (if not delayed at briefing), and the bombardier. Soon, the airfield and all the countryside around it echo with the roar of two hundred

"It was rough on the ground crew, when their plane didn't come back. They'd worked all night long getting it ready, and you'd see them waiting. It really hurt them. They had a relationship with the crew, and they have to start all over with a new crew, new plane."

Ken Stone, ball turret gunner, 381BG.

Wright R-1820 engines, 1,200 horsepower each, warming up for flight. On a signal from the tower, the airplanes roll out of the hard-stands and, in sequence according to the traffic plan, twist and turn along the perimeter track to the checkered trailer beside the takeoff point.

With the engines idling and the airplanes trembling like greyhounds in the slips, the lead pilots wait for a green light from the tower. Tense at their stations, the crewmen cannot help but think of what the next few hours will bring. Too late now to wish you'd gone on sick call, too late now to wish you hadn't joined the Air Force; this is why they gave you the rank and silver wings.

The Aldis lamp shines green; the first airplane in line moves forward and swings onto the runway, heading into wind. Holding the brakes on, the pilot guns the engines one last time. A group of well-wishers, gathered by the trailer, wave and wish the crew a safe return. Slowly gaining pace, the big bomber makes its run. At the moment when the airspeed needle comes around to takeoff speed, or the pilot's instinct tells him that the plane will fly, he gently pulls the yoke back and the mission has begun . . .

For the night bombers' takeoffs, it was much the same procedure, although movements on the airfield, usually in darkness, were necessarily laborious and slow. Cir-

Sometimes gentle, sometimes capricious, sometimes awful, never the same for two moments together; almost human in its passions, almost spiritual in its tenderness, almost Divine in its infinity.

—from "The Sky," by John Ruskin

below: A study of *Sugar Puss*, a B-17F on a dispersal hardstand-somewhere in England.

There's villainous news abroad.

—from *Henry IV*, Part I, Act II, Sc. 4, by William Shakespeare

A briefing of the 93BG
at Hardwick, Norfolk.

cumnavigation of the long perimeter track, marked by the dim, blue glim-lamps, widely spaced, called for careful use of outboard engines in conjunction with the rudders and the brakes (unlike the USAAF bombers' braking systems, those in British heavies were not differential). The bomb-aimer could help by shining an Aldis lamp on the near side of the taxiway, but every pilot knew that one wheel off the tarmac, sinking in the mud, could bring the whole squadron to a halt. Arriving safely at the caravan/trailer, he still had the problem of steering down the runway with no centerline to see. Once airborne, however, all he had to do was to keep on climbing as high as he could go, avoiding other aircraft—also climbing in their hundreds—on the way.

For the Eighth Air Force pilot, at this point in the mission, the hardest part had yet to come: he had to find the lead plane of his squadron and take his station in the combat box formation. "One time when we were assembling," Charles Bosshardt remembered, "it was still so dark you could hardly see the other ships. There were ships everywhere going in all directions. The pilot had the tail gunner flashing the Aldis lamp from his turret and the top gunner had the trouble light on making himself a lighthouse. The sunrise was beautiful. There was a narrow band of flaming red between the black sea and the clouds. And as it gradually grew lighter the clouds rolled in lower and lower and finally the mission was called off."

"You had to rally with all the other groups," said Larry Bird. "The wing would assemble, and then another wing, and finally after about an hour of this you would be ready to start moving in one big stream. You were on your way across the water, and by the time you reached Holland it was daylight. You could see this long strip of sand. And clouds, always clouds everywhere."

Road and rail communications were the targets for the bombers in mid April 1944; on Easter Monday, 166 Squadron's Lancasters lined up on the taxiway at Kirmington in Lincolnshire for an attack on the railway yards at Aulnoye. Four aircraft took off safely but the fifth swung off the runway, the pilot overcorrected, and the wheels collapsed. The instant detonation of nine tons of high explosive made a crater fifty feet in diameter and fifteen in depth. Pieces of the Lancaster flew in all directions, and a watching officer reported that a Merlin engine had missed his head by inches. By six o'clock next morning, the runway was repaired and, that evening, the squadron joined an attack on Aachen.

As the Eighth Air Force multiplied, putting more and more bombers in the air on every mission, the pilots often had difficulty in finding their lead planes, especially when the visibility was poor. The lead crews fired signal cartridges of prearranged colors over the assembly points, but as Colonel Dale O. Smith of the 384th Bomb Group observed: "When you look for the leader he isn't firing flares, and when someone in your plane sees them, by the time he calls you, the flares are out and all you see is two trails of smoke where the leader was a few minutes ago."

Nine of us rode in a weapons carrier out around the five-mile perimeter track to a dispersal point where, surrounded at a distance by vague, lumpish trees and shrubs, our ship huddled in the mist like a great dark sea lion among some wave-worn rocks. When the carrier stopped, our sergeants lifted out their guns and parked them for the moment on the engine tarps which the line crew had stacked on the grass beside the hardstand. And now, as I walked with my crewmates across the hardstand toward *The Body*, I had all my usual symptoms of pre-strike anxiety. . . . We walked toward the ship through nacreous pools of oily water on the asphalt parking area. Visibility was less than a hundred yards. We couldn't begin to see *Erector Set* and *Finah Than Dinah*, the Forts that were parked on hardstands on either side of ours on the perimeter. It was stations time, a quarter to ten, and we went into *The Body*. The pearly ground fog had lifted; low clouds were running down to the eastward like suds in a rocky river bed. From my seat in the cockpit I could see the cubical control tower in the far distance, and I could even make out some tiny figures— members of the operational staff—on the iron-railed balcony of the tower. Eight or ten Forts were visible, scattered at their hardstands along the perimeter track, dark and squat, imponderable, rooted to the ground by their tail wheels. A big camouflaged R.A.F. gasoline lorry and trailer moved slowly along the main road toward the hangars. . . . I pressed the starter button for number one, and I could hear the whine of the inertia starter in the wing. I unlocked the

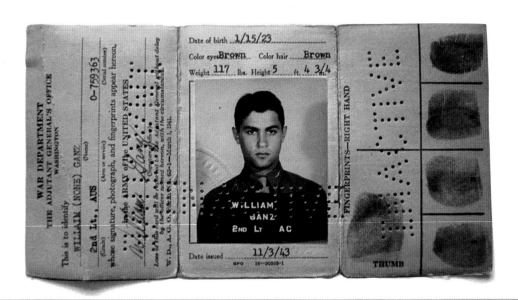

above: The A.G.O. card of 2/Lt.William Ganz, a co-pilot in the 398BG at Nuthampstead, south of Cambridge, below: The runway and hangars at RAF Dishforth, Yorkshire, above right: Bicycle tire supports at RAF Syerston, right: T2 hangar doors at Syerston in 1992.

primer and set it to number one and pumped up a solid charge of fuel . . . and I flipped the switch to mesh and craned and saw the momentary burst of blue smoke sweep out into the prop wash as number one caught and we heard the roar and felt the shaking of all that energy. We went to work on number two.

—from *The War Lover*, by John Hersey

above: An RAF bomber pilot and his flight engineer, right: Col.Dale O. Smith, Commanding Officer of the 384BG at Grafton Underwood in 1944, above right: *The Tweacherous Wabbit* lifts from a Lavenham runway in June 1944, far right: A 44BG officer at Shipdham observes B-24s of his group as they return from a raid.

"The forests over there are very stable, and they're protected. They've had the same outline for centuries. They're real jealous of their woods over there. They put them on the maps, and they're identifiable by their shape—one of the salient features you can use for pilot navigation."

Lawrence Drew, pilot, 384BG

Though this be madness, yet there is method in't.

—from *Hamlet*, Act II, Sc. 2, by William Shakespeare

Dale Smith's answer was to have his lead crews fire a constant stream of flares, and to keep on firing them until the squadrons formed. Another solution adopted by the Eighth was to deploy brightly painted airplanes—usually the war-weary B-17s or B-24s—which, having served as airborne assembly points, returned to their bases when the wings had formed.

Assembling the airplanes into elements of three, the elements into squadrons, the squadrons into groups, and the groups into combat wings, called for careful timing and precision flying. By the time Ira Eaker's vision of bombing round the clock had become a reality, the Eighth had devised a method which, however laborious it may seem to us now, had the advantage that it worked. On one mission, for example, the targets were railroad yards and tank plants in Berlin. Over East Anglia, the base of the cloud was at 3,000 feet and the tops were at 6,000. On forty Eighth Air Force bases, the takeoffs began at 7:00 A.M., and the bombers followed one another into the air at sixty-second intervals. Then each pilot headed for the Buncher—his group radio beacon—some twelve miles away, made a full turn around it, and flew a climbing racetrack pattern between the Buncher and the Splasher base beacon until he reached clear air.

Once above the cloud tops, flying in wide circles around the Bunchers, the squadrons took their places in the group formations and, at eight-fifteen, the group lead pilots turned out of their orbits and headed for the wing assembly points, flying dogleg

courses that could be shortened or extended to allow the other group formations to fit in. From the wing assembly points, still on dog-leg courses, the bombers converged to form divisions above the Norfolk coast. Almost two hours to the minute since the first take-offs began, the people of Cromer heard the muffled thunder as 450 B-17s of the 1st Air Division passed above their town. A few miles to the south, 350 B-24s of the 2nd Air Division roared across Great Yarmouth while, over Southwold on the Suffolk coast, 530 of the 3rd Air Division's B-17s turned to join the great armada heading for "Big B."

It didn't always work out quite like that. "Our first combat mission was a sort of farce," revealed Bill Ganz of the 398th Bomb Group. "There was heavy overcast, and we had trouble forming in the group. Eventually we picked up a group that was headed east and tagged along." W. W. Ford of the 92nd had a similar experience: "We made two orbits of the beacon and we weren't picking anybody up. We'd been briefed to go on after a certain time if that happened, but when we broke out of the cloud around 22,000 feet there wasn't another airplane anywhere in sight. Over the coast of France we picked up a lead plane from our group and formed up on him. In the next twenty minutes we picked up a B-24 from the 2nd Air Division and three more B-17s from all over. We went on to Munich with this bunch, made the bomb run, and came back in formation. As soon as we hit the English coast everybody said, 'Good-bye, nice flying with you.'"

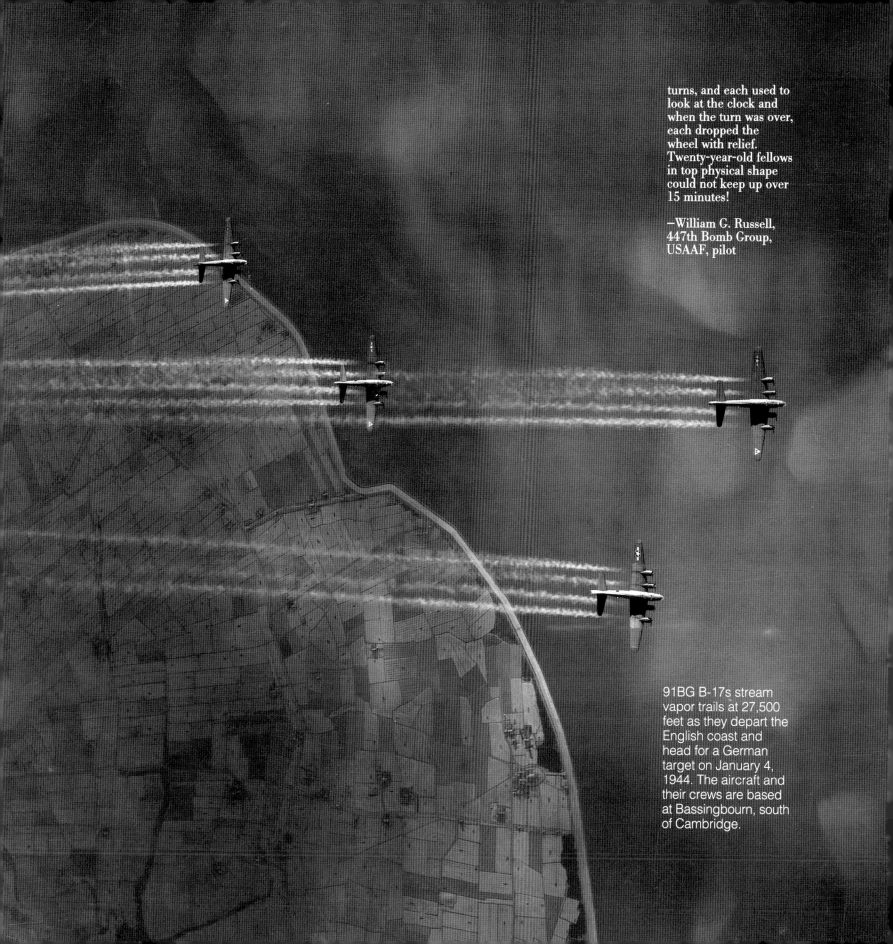

turns, and each used to look at the clock and when the turn was over, each dropped the wheel with relief. Twenty-year-old fellows in top physical shape could not keep up over 15 minutes!

—William G. Russell, 447th Bomb Group, USAAF, pilot

91BG B-17s stream vapor trails at 27,500 feet as they depart the English coast and head for a German target on January 4, 1944. The aircraft and their crews are based at Bassingbourn, south of Cambridge.

BASE ROUTINE

... Air Ministry teams surveyed the place and pronounced it suitable for a Bomber Command airfield. After that came earth-moving machinery, concrete mixers and asphalt pourers. A tarmac cross was drawn across (the) countryside and around it went a road complete with a circular pan for each airplane. Men dug sewers and drains, laid water pipes and strung power lines. Telex and phone cables crossed the fields. Corrugated-iron Nissen huts appeared as if by magic, huddled together like wrinkled gray elephants sheltering from the cold East Anglian winds. There were hangars too: black cathedrals higher than the church steeple and wider than the graveyard. Finally out of the clouds came the sound of an airplane and ten minutes later [it] was truly an airfield. The boxlike control tower stood alone. Behind it dozens of buildings provided the complex necessities of service life from A to Z. Armory, Butchery, Cinema, Dental Surgery, Equipment Store, Flying Control, Gunnery Range, Hairdresser, Instrument Section, Jail, Kitchens,

MOST EIGHTH AIR FORCE MEN were given a week or two to get accustomed to life on an English airfield before they were committed to the fight. Ray Wild, who arrived at Podington, Bedfordshire, to join the 92nd Bomb Group in September 1943, remembered his induction: "What they did when you showed up at the field, they had you shoot some landings, they checked out your crew, and they assigned you to a squadron. I ended up with the 325th. They had a wall with names on it—twelve missions, fourteen missions—and MIA, KIA. None of us knew what that meant. They showed you that and then they took you to the ready room, and you took your crew out flying formation for a short period of time, according to how fast they needed replacement crews to fly missions."

During this period of orientation, while they were flying cross-countries, learning to use the gee-box, dropping practice bombs, attending classroom studies (and learning that the letters on the wall meant "missing in action" and "killed in action"), the rule in some groups was that new arrivals were restricted to the base. "I was paid today in one-pound notes," Keith Newhouse noted at Rackheath, "I have a roll to choke a horse with and can do nothing with it. Can't buy a thing but a week's rations at the PX. We sit here and grow restless. We've been confined too long."

Ray Wild had won his wings at Moody Field, Valdosta, Georgia—"Mother Moody's Rest Camp" as it was sometimes known. Officially, Wild should not have been a pilot: on enlistment he was just six months too old.

But he had lied a little, made a careful alteration to his birth certificate, and for all the Air Force knew, he was eighteen months inside the limit. The things he remembered best about his time at Podington were all evoked by odors. "The first time it hit me was in that ready room. It was damp, musty—it had probably been that way for months. Then when you went into the briefing hut, and the briefing officers checked you out, you would always smell shaving lotion on those guys. It bothered the hell out of me. You had these heavy boots, heavy pants and jackets, and you opened them up and there was body smell then—not really unpleasant, but not pleasant because it was connected with the raid.

"Then we might sit waiting in the airplane for thirty, forty minutes, and there was a heavy smell of gasoline, but there was a ready room smell in there, too, every time. I guess it was the odor of fear. On the runway, and for the first thousand feet or so, there'd still be the gasoline, and the smell of burnt cordite from the Channel on. Coming back, we'd take off the mask and smoke a cigarette, and there was that smell, and always the cold sweat smell, until we got back on the ground. But after we landed, there was no gasoline smell, no cordite, no sweat—nothing that wasn't nice. It was all connected with fear and non-fear, I guess."

By the time W. W. Ford arrived at Podington in February 1945, Wild had not only completed his tour of missions with the 92nd, but had also undertaken another kind of tour: selling War Loan bonds in the States

Thanksgiving dinner at
Great Ashfield in 1943.

Link Trainer Room, Meteorological Section, Navigator's Briefing Room, Operations Block, Photographic Section, Quarters for Married Officers, Radar Building, Sick Quarters, Teleprinter Section, Uniform Store, Vehicle Repair Yard, Water Tower, X-Ray Department, Y.M.C.A. hut, and a zebra-striped Aerodrome Control Post.

—from *Bomber*, by Len Deighton

"The heads were about forty yards up a hill, and on a cold, snowy night it was agony to go. That's why the snow was pure yellow at the front door of the hut."

John B. Thomas, copilot, 446BG

"I was walking along a road on the base and I saw this truck approaching driven by a big black dog. Then I remembered that in England the drivers sat on the opposite side to American drivers. That dog was a passenger."

Charles J. Bosshardt, navigator, 458BG

far left: The water tower at RAF Wymeswold, center left: A WAAF as painted by Dame Laura Knight in 1940, above left: A crew hut remaining at Knettishall, Norfolk, below left: A mural still on a wall at Bungay, Suffolk, below: Jack Loman's art in Shipdham's cookhouse.

with Bing Crosby and Bob Hope. At Podington, the air war still went on. Three days after joining the 92nd, Ford's crew attended a dummy briefing session in the operations room. "It was fairly late when we finished, and we were about to be dismissed when the planes on that day's mission started coming back. One had been hit pretty badly, and they pulled up in front of Operations because it was the closest place to the hospital. The copilot and the tail gunner had been wounded, and a piece of flak had come through the nose and taken most of the back of the bombardier's head off. They unloaded these guys right in front of us, and it was a gory mess. That was our introduction to the way it was in combat."

"We would make runs in formation," said Lawrence Drew, "on fictitious targets in England, get back to the base, and make some instrument approaches and landings for hours—just touch the wheels down, give it the gun, go around, and come back for another. All the time there was something to do—work on your radio operator's speed, your engineer's knowhow—there was always training to do. We carried a very high fatigue factor at that time. If I had five minutes in a chow line I could go to sleep standing up."

The grind of training continued long after the preliminary phase; in fact, it never stopped. "When you weren't flying a mission," said Paul Sink, "you were flying a practice mission or going to class or something. You didn't have much spare time. That was for psychological reasons: if you didn't have time to think, you didn't have

far left: Lt.Ray Wild, center, standing, and the crew of *Mizpah*, a 92BG B17. The plane was one of nine that Lt.Wild flew during his 30-mission tour at Podington. All of his aircraft were named *Mizpah*, left: The tower at Flixton, Suffolk, below: The technical site at Flixton.

below and right: B-17 memorabilia found since WWII on the disused airfield at Grafton Underwood, center right: Ground crewmen gather empty .50 caliber shell cases from a B-17 after its return from a mission to Stuttgart, center below: Flight nurse 2/Lt Martha Radspieler, at Knettishall.

time to get nervous, and if you didn't get nervous you were a better flier."

Part of the routine for the ground crew, and for many of the fliers not assigned to the mission, was to count the bombers coming home and watch them land. The top brass would assemble on the balcony of the control tower and sometimes on the roof. This was undoubtedly the best vantage point but not always the safest place to be. On March 17, 1945, the 493rd Bomb Group, having

"I don't think I'll be warm until I get home. The coal here is rationed and the stoves are just bulges in the chimney, not to warm us up, but to keep us from freezing to death. Paper is rationed, too, so going to the toilet needs a search for some material."

Keith Newhouse, pilot, 467BG

60

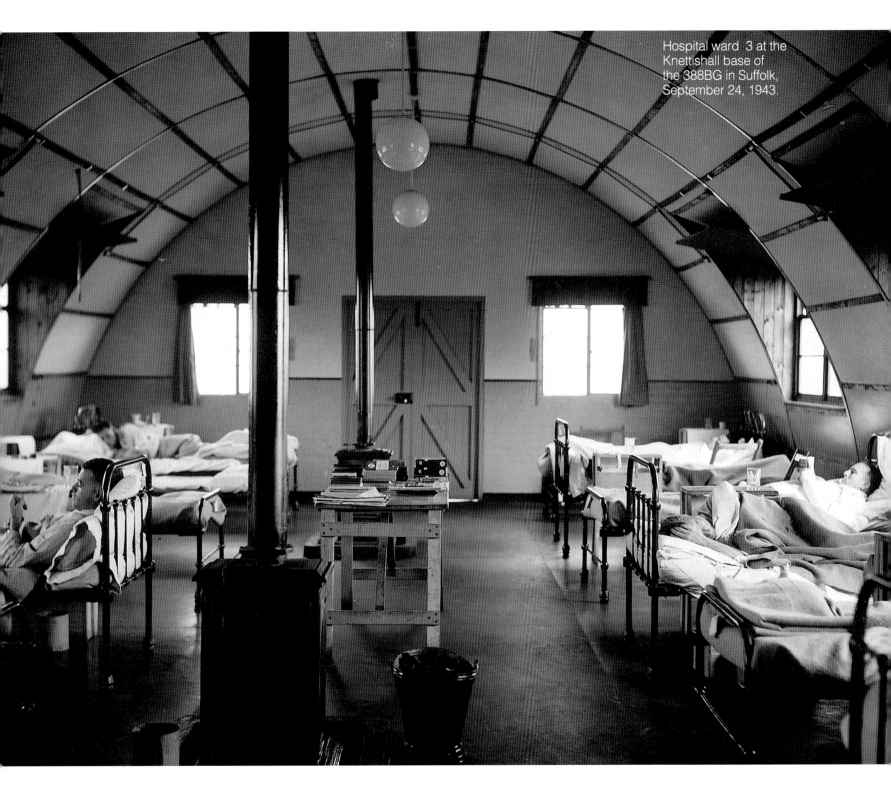

Hospital ward 3 at the Knettishall base of the 388BG in Suffolk, September 24, 1943.

61

climbed above the cumulus to attack oil installations north of Leipzig, returned to find their airfield weathered in. "We were expecting a five-hundred-foot cloud base at Debach," said rear gunner Paul Sink, "but it was a whole lot lower than that when we got back. I heard the copilot say, 'I see the runway,' and we started letting down, but then the pilot said, 'It's the goddamned control tower.' We cleared that thing by inches, and

"We didn't often eat breakfast in the sergeants' mess. We used to cycle to a farmhouse down the road, and the farmer's wife would give us fried egg in a bread roll and a cup of tea for sixpence. There was a queue there most mornings."

Jim Barfoot, mid-upper gunner, 207 Sqn.

above: ARC donut girls, right: Hardwick ground personnel on a coffee break, above right: 93BG bomb handlers at work.

"I was the youngest in the crew and the only Englishman. When the going was tough, the Aussies were the chaps you needed with you. They had guts, they never gave in."

Jack Clift, flight engineer, 463 Sqn.

top: Air traffic control staff in the 93BG tower at Hardwick, above: Intelligence personnel at RAF Pocklington.

top left: 93BG aircrew members at ease in their Hardwick Nissen hut, top right: 493BG parachute store, far right: The parachute store at RAF Marston Moor, home to various heavy bomber units including 617 (Dambusters) Squadron.

all of the people on it were jumping overboard."

From 1941 onward, British airfields were never subjected to the sort of constant harassment inflicted on Luftwaffe bases by Mosquitoes and Marauders, but they were not immune from enemy intruders. Armorer Sam Burchell, whose task at Seething was to load B-24 Liberators of the 448th with bullets and with bombs, remembered an attack in 1944. "They came in under the radar at the same time as the planes were coming home in the afternoon. They really did a job of strafing our base. Some people did get hurt and there were bombs going off and machine guns and everything. That was the only time I saw what you might call combat. Of course, the aircrews saw it every day."

Always, following a mission, there would be lots of questions in the operations block—interrogation, or debriefing, as it was later called. The airmen would be given something to relax them: cigarettes on the table, cocoa and a tot of rum for the RAF, coffee and perhaps a slug of scotch or brandy for the USAAF. The men who didn't care for alcohol would sometimes pass their ration to the ones who did. The crews, often weary and not always quite coherent, were questioned by officers of the int./ops branch.

"Did you hit the target?" the RAF men would be asked. "Was the marking good? Did you see the route markers? Were you attacked—where, and what action did you take? Did you see any aircraft go down, and where?" The USAAF crews were similarly quizzed. "Was the formation tight? Did you

bomb the primary? Where did you encounter flak, where fighters? When this or that plane went down, how many chutes did you see?" Elsewhere in the operations block, there would be separate debriefings for the force commanders and lead pilots, navigators and bombardiers. From the answers to their questions, the debriefers would collate their raid reports and send them up the wire for analysis at wing or group HQ.

At most USAAF bases there was also a postoperational critique. The photographs of the target would be displayed and the group commander would make his observations. "Whenever they turned the lights out to show the strike photos," commented Charles Bosshardt of the 458th, "we would stretch out on the benches and nap. Our buddies would punch us to wake us up when the lights came on again. The critiques were a pain. We were all tired out and the colonel would be harping on some failure to follow his instructions. I recall that he talked once about the loose formation. He said he could have flown his P-51 through it. One of the pilots spoke up and said, 'Well, hell, Colonel, I could have flown through too if I had a little plane like that.'"

Everyone quickly got accustomed to the sudden disappearance of roommates from the scene. "It was a bit upsetting sometimes," said Jack Clift. "You'd just get off to sleep and the RAF Police would come in and go through their lockers, load all their gear into kit bags, take it out, and that's the last you'd see of them. They'd never be spoken of. We'd never talk about them after that."

ON AUGUST 17, 1943, just one year to the day since Ira Eaker and his twelve B-17s flew the opening USAAF mission of the European war, a force of thirty times that number—the largest yet assembled—made the first American deep-penetration sorties into the heart of Germany. In 1942, the objective had been barely forty miles from the Channel coast of France: the anniversary targets—the Messerschmitt factory in Regensburg and the ball-bearing plants in Schweinfurt—were both in Bavaria, and the route to the farthest passed over four hundred miles of hostile territory.

The attacks were planned to begin simultaneously—at ten minutes before 12:00 noon—with the aim of splitting the fighter opposition, but, as every fighting man knows, few plans survive exposure to the enemy, and in this case, the enemy was aided by the weather. The skies over Regensburg were reported to be clear, while Schweinfurt was obscured by ten-tenths cloud. To the RAF bomber crews, that would have mattered little: using radar marking, they would have rained the bombs down just the same. Not so the Eighth: at that stage of the war, Pinetree's edict was that bombardiers must see their targets.

On the Regensburg mission, 146 B-17s of the 4th Bomb Wing, flying in three combat box formations, were escorted by P-47s as far as the Belgian frontier. From there on, the bombers were subjected to a persistent onslaught by relays of fighters with cannon fire and rockets. The Luftwaffe mounted a formidable defense: Messerschmitt 109s, 110s, and 210s, Focke-Wulf 190s, and Junkers 88s rose in their hundreds to repel the bombers. In the Fortresses, the intercoms crackled with urgent admonitions: "Fire short bursts. . . . Don't waste rounds. . . . Lead 'em more." At times, it seemed to observers that the sky was filled with the debris of aerial combat: pieces of airplane, both American and German, life rafts and fuel tanks, exit doors and hatches. Some men fell with parachutes, other men without. Black smoke columns towered from burning bombers in the fields below.

After ninety minutes, the fighters broke away. Their controllers planned to reengage the bombers on return. The B-17s swept on to Regensburg and, flying in the height band between 17,000 and 18,000 feet, released three hundred tons of bombs. The strike on the factory was well concentrated, and the results achieved by the 390th Bomb Group, in particular, of 58 percent strikes within 1,000 feet of the aiming point and 94 percent inside 2,000 feet, were precision bombing of a high order.

Two months earlier, sixty Lancasters of No. 5 Group, having attacked a radar assembly plant on the north shore of Lake Constance, had flown on across the Alps and the Mediterranean Sea to land in Algeria. Three nights later, refueled and reloaded for the homeward flight, they had bombed the Italian naval base at La Spezia en route. That small force of Lancasters had flown the first shuttle mission of the war: the 4th Bomb Wing of the Eighth Air Force now embarked upon the second. Twenty-four aircraft had

"Doesn't this world ever make you want to throw up, Doc?" "Constantly." "Once upon a time," he said, "there was a crow with the appetite of a condor, or perhaps a goat. It didn't care how things tasted, but only how they looked. It liked bright objects, silver and shining blue things, and one day it ate a lady's ring, a nickel a child had lost by the roadside, a priest's collar button, a sequin, a violinist's mute, a juke-box slug, and a lot of other junk like that. In the afternoon the crow began to feel nauseated, and he said to himself, 'Must be something I ate.' His crop got more and more uncomfortable, and finally he oopsed everything. The morsels he had thrown up looked so pretty that he wanted to eat them all over again, but believing that one of them had made him sick he decided not to eat any of them at all, and he flew away with a sense of forfeited pleasure. Do you know what the moral of this fable is?" "Don't eat breakfast before going on a mission," I said. "Wrong," Doc said. "The moral is: People don't know what's bad for them until after the fun's gone out of it." "Doc," I said, "You're the God-damnedest man I ever met."

—from *The War Lover*, by John Hersey

below: An 8AF B-17 is shown returning from a raid, in this painting by Frank Wootton, above right: Marvin T.Lord, below right: Ken Stone, page 66: A wounded crew member being assisted from his B-17 at Kimbolton.

gone down; the survivors landed safely on airstrips in North Africa.

Three hours after the attack on Regensburg had ended, the 1st Bomb Wing's force of more than two hundred B-17s made their delayed approach on Schweinfurt, 120 miles to the northwest. Ken Stone, at twenty years of age, was manning the ball turret of the 381st Bomb Group's *Big Time Operator:* "I was awakened at three o'clock in the morning by the operations officer at Ridgewell, Captain Robert Nelson. I ate a hearty breakfast and rode out to the briefing room. Then I cleaned and dried my guns in the armament shack and installed them in the ball turret. I donned my flying clothes and sat down and waited until the officers came out at five-forty-five. Our plane was lead ship and our regular pilot, Lieutenant Lord, was flying as tail gunner to check the formation. Captain Briggs was flying as pilot and Major Hall as copilot. They started the engines at six o'clock and warmed them up. The control tower called and delayed takeoff one hour due to weather over the target. The engines were restarted at seven o'clock but before taxi-time they delayed the mission again. I took a nap and the roar of the engines woke me up at nine o'clock. Then a red flare was fired from control and the mission was once more delayed. A truck came out with some Spam sandwiches. I managed to eat two of them . . ."

Marvin T. Lord's crew had first become acquainted with the *Big Time Operator* at Pueblo, Colorado, while they were undergoing the final phase of their training. They

had flown her to England, and on sixteen missions since they joined the 381st. Stone liked the airplane, and he liked his pilot; he particularly liked his pilot's name. "I'm flying with the Lord," he used to tell himself, "and the Lord will protect me."

Big Time Operator eventually took off at eleven-thirty. Stone entered the ball turret, and the group's twenty B-17s formed up over England with the rest of the wing. Again, the "little friends" gave cover to the limit of their range, but from Aachen onward the bombers flew alone. Refueled and rearmed, the German fighters were ready; so was Stone. "I watched them circle our group, sizing us up, and then they came in line abreast, with guns blazing. The first pass, they came head-on at us, and it was the first time they'd done this. It was something new to us, and very effective. Then they flew underneath our plane and into the formation. They were Me 109s and Fw 190s that were hitting us. I had plenty of good shots, but I don't know if I got any—I was too busy shooting at the next one coming in—but I'm sure I didn't waste all my ammunition. Lord said one blew up after it passed us, and he figured I might have gotten it. Two wing men were hit—Painter on our left and Jarvis on our right. The waist gunners waved to us and then they went down. Lieutenant Darrow's plane had an engine knocked out, but he managed to keep up with the formation. After what seemed like hours, the fighters disappeared.

"We were met," Stone went on, "by a medium amount of flak over the target. That

"It wasn't always the long trips that were the worst. Sometimes we got more flak near the English coast than we did over the target. That was the Royal Navy. It didn't matter what we did—shoot off the colors of the day and everything—the Navy always fired at us."

Leonard Thompson, flight engineer, 550 sqn.

"We blew hell out of the target yesterday. Visibility was good, so we had a good run although there was some confusion lining up. Coming back it was dark and clouded. Jerry was raising hell at our field when we arrived. It was the first time we had to fight our way in. Through lack of gas, enemy planes, and the British ack-ack there were B-24s crashing all over England. The four officers who have shared our barracks were killed in a crash landing a short way from the field. It adds up to the fact that no one knows when he is in for curtains. As the RAF say, 'He's had it.' A lot of fellows 'had it' last evening."

Keith Newhouse, pilot, 467BG

"Over Berlin, I saw an 88-mm shell come up, and I just sat there for maybe two or three seconds from the time it stopped rising until it started dropping, just sort of hanging in the air, suspended. As it started dropping it exploded. Yeah, you could see them once in a while."

Larry Bird, toggleer, 493BG

was the scariest thing—when you had to go over the target and your bombardier controlled the plane. You had to fly steady, and you could see what you were headed into. It didn't deter our bombardier, Lieutenant Hester. He dropped his bombs and the other planes dropped theirs. The bomb bay doors were right in front of me, and I could always watch the bombs. I watched them fall all the way. It seemed like Hester hit the factory itself. The whole target was well plastered and the smoke rose high. Lieutenant Darrow was still clinging on. I knew it wouldn't be long before the fighters returned. The tension was very great.

"Fifteen minutes later, the fighters were sighted coming in from our right. I thought, this is it. I never thought I'd make it back that day. I was really scared, and I prayed to God to get me through this. They circled us once, lined up, and attacked head-on again. Chutes were going down all over the sky, brown ones and white ones: it looked like an airborne invasion. The fighters kept on coming in, passing under and coming around again. The odds were against us. It's not like in the movies, when you hear the fighters zooming and all the sound effects. You just hear your own airplane, and its engines. And you hear your own guns.

"At last the fighters left us. We flew on for about fifteen more minutes, then I saw fighters miles to our left and heading our way. We said, 'Uh-oh, here we go again,' but they turned out to be our escort. They were angels from heaven. I turned the turret around: there were ten planes left in the

group. Lieutenant Darrow was dragging along on two engines, and dropping out to our left. It looked like he would have to ditch in the Channel. The white cliffs of Dover were the most beautiful sight in the world, and ten minutes later, when I got out of the turret, I was the happiest person in all the world. *Big Time Operator* had pulled us through again. We were safe, and back in good old England."

The German fighter planes had shot down twenty-one B-17s en route to the target, and destroyed fourteen more on the homeward flight. Although the target defenses were described by seasoned crews as negligible, yet another bomber fell to the Schweinfurt flak. The Eighth had lost more aircraft in a day than in its first six months of operations.

That night, Air Chief Marshal Harris sent six hundred heavies to attack the Baltic rocket base at Peenemünde. It was the opening gambit in the Allied air campaign, later code-named *Crossbow*, which would be waged against the factories and launching sites of the enemy's "V-weapons."

The 4th Bomb Wing, returning from North Africa seven days later and attacking Bordeaux airfield on the way, was grievously depleted. In addition to the aircraft lost attacking Regensburg, another twelve had suffered damage beyond the resources of the African outposts to repair, and three were missing from the shuttle operation over France. For its fight against the odds, the whole wing received a Distinguished Unit Citation, and Major Gale Cleven of the 100th

No words could adequately express our admiration and appreciation for the American escort pilots. Few of us in the 8th Bomber Command would have escaped either oblivion or a prison camp in 1943 without their help.

—from *Combat Crew*, by John Comer

left: 357FG P-51B and D Mustang escort fighters.

below: Interrogation at plane-side following an attack on Northern France, June 12, 1944.

Is your life worth 1.000 bucks ?

No !

It's not worth 10 cents since you have left « God's own country » and come to Europe, to get killed in battle.

Honestly now !

Do you know why you are fighting us ? — Formerly, you were glad enough to take a trip to Europe on our big boats, and we were good friends until Roosevelt, Churchill and Stalin drove us into war.

You've got to die for F. D. R.

Don't you realize it's only for Roosevelt's re-election.

You've got to die for Churchill.

So that the English plutocrats, who own half the world, may haul in more money.

You've got to die for Stalin.

So that Bolshevist murderers should light the brand of revolution in your own land.

THINK OF THE TEARS OF THOSE YOU LEFT AT HOME.

So long as you keep on fighting, you have nothing but death to look forward to.

Come over to us, you will be treated well and in a friendly manner !

Come to us and you will certainly some day embrace your loved ones again and live your young life as you are entitled to do.

AW 50

above: Nazi propaganda leaflet, right: portrait of a Luftwaffe pilot.

Bomb Group, leading the rear formation, which had borne the brunt of the enemy attacks, was awarded the Distinguished Service Cross.

Throughout the dire Regensburg and Schweinfurt operations, the conduct of the crews could not be criticized: they had met the fighter onslaught with enormous courage. The Flying Fortress gunners had hit back with everything they had, and although the early claims were optimistic, as they often could be in the heat of battle (a Messerschmitt came in, many guns were fired at it, and, at the debriefing, several gunners claimed the kill), twenty-five of their attackers had been shot out of the sky. Both the main targets had been accurately bombed, but so efficient were the Germans at rehabilitation that the factories resumed production in a week and were almost back to normal in two months.

Assessed, therefore, as bombing operations, the attacks could be looked upon as qualified successes: in terms of economy in men and machinery, they could not be so regarded. Five hundred young Americans were missing in action somewhere over Europe, and many homecoming aircraft had carried dead and wounded. Over 31 percent of the bombers had been lost, and others had suffered heavy battle damage. These were savage blows—as savage as any the RAF had taken in the early days—and the Eighth reverted to short-range targets for a while. The next big encounter with the enemy defenses came on September 6, and was as costly as the last. The aiming point in Stuttgart was hidden under cloud, few crews found the primary target, and forty-five aircraft were lost in the attempt. Five more, with battle damage, were forced to land in Switzerland; another twenty-one, short of fuel, ditched or crash-landed in England.

Again, the Eighth stepped back and took a breath. For a few weeks, most of the targets selected for the bombers were in France or on the German North Sea coast. In the next four thousand sorties ninety planes were lost, and a third of these went down on the only long-range mission: an attack on Münster's railways and canals. Eaker then decided that General Anderson's bombers must return to Schweinfurt and its three ball-bearing plants. On October 14, the crews were briefed for the follow-up attack. At Great Ashfield, Lieutenant Colonel Vandervanter spoke a few words of encouragement to the 385th Bomb Group. "This is a tough job," he told "Van's Valiants," "but I know you can do it. Good luck, good bombing, good hunting . . ." From the seated ranks in the briefing room, a lone voice added ". . . and good-bye."

The 1st and 3rd Bomb Divisions dispatched three hundred B-17s to the primary target, while B-24s of the 2nd Bomb Division made a diversionary attack on Emden. Ray Wild was flying his third mission out of Podington with the 92nd Bomb Group. "We were off to an early start. We reached altitude and got over the French coast. Somehow, we failed to pick up the low group of our wing. As we were lead wing, the colonel decided we had better fall in with another

73

group. We did a three-sixty over the Channel and, seeing fifteen planes ahead of us that didn't seem to be attached to anyone, we just tagged along with them. We picked up enemy fighters at just about the time our own escort had to leave. From that moment, it was unbelievable. For three hours over enemy territory, we had fighters shooting tracer and rockets at us. You could see those rockets coming. They were about eighteen inches long, and when they hit they would explode and set the plane on fire. Some twin-engine jobs at about a thousand feet above us were dropping bombs on the formation. There was no way they could aim at any one bomber—they were just dropping bombs into the group. And they were dropping chains or cables to foul our propellers.

"We were riding Ray Clough's left wing when he got hit. He dropped out, and twenty seconds later he burst into flames. Brown got hit and disintegrated: a great sheet of flame and then a hole in the formation. I took over the lead of the second element just prior to going over the target. Major Ott was riding on three engines and had to drop behind. I never saw him again. Even over the target, the fighters came on through the flak. It was one of the few times they did that. They were really first team, those guys. They had guts and they were damned good fliers. They'd come in close, and if you straggled by as much as fifty yards, you'd had it. You'd get hit by three or four guys.

"The main thing was, the lead bombardier did a beautiful job on the target, but about three minutes later we got hit in number three engine. Due to loss of the prop governor control we couldn't feather it, and we began to sweat. We had to use maximum manifold pressure and 2,500 revs to stay in formation. We limped home as far as the Channel and started to let down into the nearest field. We got into Biggin Hill, southeast of London. Seven Forts set down there and they were all shot up. Several had wounded aboard and one had a dead navigator. We had fifteen holes in the ship and only about sixty gallons of gas left. After Schweinfurt, I thought the rest would seem easy."

The return to Schweinfurt had been yet another calamitous event: sixty B-17s had failed to return, more than twice that number had suffered battle damage, and over six hundred officers and men were missing, dead, or wounded.

It could have been a deathblow for precision daylight bombing; indeed, a partial switch to night bombing was considered for a while. At the end of the day, however, the USAAF commanders held fast to their philosophy, while the operations staff at Pinetree undertook a total tactical reappraisal. Stuttgart had indicated the need for pathfinder aircraft, equipped with a version—a better one if possible—of the RAF's H2S radar; all the long-range missions had shown a requirement for more firepower for the bombers and protection for the crews; the combat box formations must be flown tighter for mutual support; above all, the range of the "little friends" had to be extended.

Meanwhile, in Germany, the armaments ministry planned a wider dispersal of

above: From the diary of Lt. Ray Wild, 92BG, 1943.

. . . they must have been a mile or so off track and had got the hammer. This is the way things are in flying; you are either lucky or you aren't.

—from *Enemy Coast Ahead,* by Guy Gibson

right: Knettishall wall art, below: The tower at RAF Waltham.

vital war industries and the urgent construction of underground factories. The Luftwaffe generals had also read the signs: despite their fearful losses, the American formations were still hitting targets and knocking down fighters, and it seemed they intended to go on. There was only one thing for it: Berlin must be told that the production of fighters should immediately be doubled, and that the training hours for pilots had to be reduced.

All these decisions, in England and in Germany, were translated into action in the ensuing months, and those that affected the USAAF fighters' range and the Luftwaffe training were to have a major impact on the outcome of the air war.

Four months later, in what was to become known as the Eighth Air Force's "Big Week," Schweinfurt was to discover what bombing round the clock meant. On February 24, 1944, the 1st Air Division, heavily escorted by P-47s and the new Merlin-engined P-51 Mustangs, all with long-range fuel tanks, struck the ball-bearing plants; that same night, Air Chief Marshal Harris, pausing briefly in the Battle of Berlin, dispatched his Lancasters and Halifaxes in two separate attacks with two thousand tons of bombs. The whirlwind had come, and the dead had been avenged.

O God assist our side: at least, avoid assisting the enemy and leave the rest to me.

—Prince Leopold of Anhalt-Dessau

left: Surviving WWII chalkboard at RAF Snaith, right: A field transfusion is given at Kimbolton.

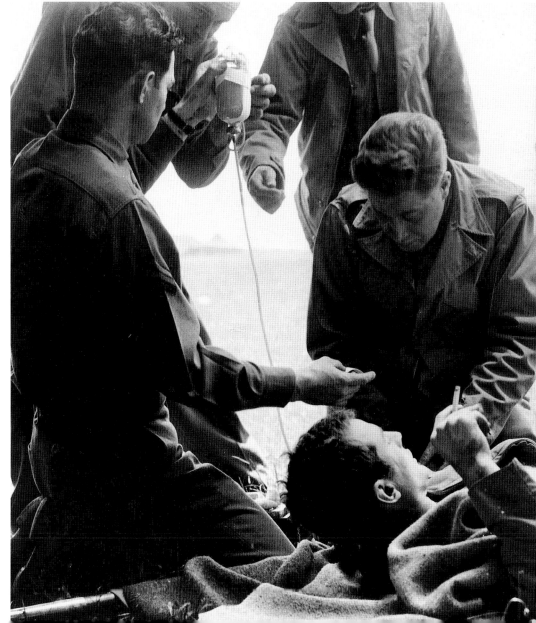

you are entering

GREAT ASHFIELD AIRDROME

Home of Van's Valiants

This is a
MILITARY RESERVATION

BASE REGULATIONS
will be OBSERVED.

VICTORIA

PREWAR RAF STATIONS were compact, brick-built settlements set close by the airfields, with neat, paved roads, squash courts and tennis courts, playing fields and cinemas, workshops and barber shops, canteens and libraries, churches and sick bays; the great "C"-type hangars, standing in a phalanx, held not only aircraft but centrally heated offices and comfortable crew rooms. You approached these bases along a tree-lined avenue, through guarded, wrought-iron gates, to arrive at the proud, gray edifice of Station Headquarters, with an RAF ensign fluttering above. The three-story messes, with ivy-covered walls, fronted by flower beds, offered spacious dining rooms, ante-rooms, billiard rooms, ladies' rooms, and quiet rooms. You would not have been surprised to find a butler's pantry. A few British, Canadian, and Australian squadrons lived on bases of this sort, and American fighter groups occupied a handful, but the only USAAF bomb groups so comfortably ensconced were the 91st at Bassingbourn near Cambridge and, at a later time, the 458th at Horsham St. Faith near Norwich.

Other bases were thrown up in a hurry to accommodate the majority of Eighth Air Force bomb groups, and to meet the expansion of both the Allied bomber commands in 1943. They were technically functional, but their facilities were primitive and their aspect was austere. They were grafted onto fields where, only weeks before, farmers had grazed cattle or raised potatoes, wheat, and barley. Their narrow roads were muddy, and the only structures over ten feet high were

the control tower, the water tower, the A.M. Bombing Teacher, the parachute store, and the far-flung "T2" hangars (no crew rooms or heating) on the fringes of the field. All the other buildings were prefabricated huts and shanty-type structures dispersed around the area as though they had been taken up and dropped as an example of saturation bombing at its worst. Strangely, many airmen preferred this type of base: perhaps it just seemed better suited to the waging of a war.

Sam Burchell's base at Seething was of the wartime sort. "Our building was a Nissen hut—just one big room for about forty of us, with one stove in the middle for which we were always trying to steal coal. It was extremely cold in the winter in that part of England, and damp. There were no separate quarters for sergeants or anything like that. Actually, everybody in the Air Force was a sergeant except me."

Of his quarters at Lissett, RAF rear gunner Fred Allen said: "We lived in a wooden hut beside a hedge two miles from the camp. There were four crews to a hut—twenty-eight people—and you got to know them pretty well. You didn't get to know many others. You slept, you flew, and the only time you weren't with your crew was when you went on leave."

When the B-24 crews of the 467th Bomb Group arrived at Rackheath in early March of 1944, the airfield contractors were still working on the base. The group was destined to fly over five thousand sorties, and to achieve the highest overall rating for accurate bombing in the Eighth; initially, how-

HOME SWEET HOME

His billet was a Nissen hut half a mile from the officers' mess. It was divided into single cubicles, each just large enough to hold a truckle bed, a chest of drawers, and a battered single wardrobe. A batman was assigned to each hut. The wash house was fifty yards away.

—from *Yesterday's Gone*, by N. J. Crisp

I could sleep. Or maybe it was a form of death. I would stretch out in the sack and feel my muscles give way completely. There was no pleasure in it. They just went flat and lifeless. And then my nerve endings would die for a while, until Porada came to wake us up.

—from *Serenade to the Big Bird*, by Bert Stiles.

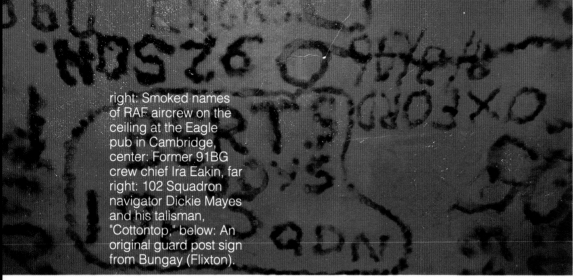

right: Smoked names of RAF aircrew on the ceiling at the Eagle pub in Cambridge. center: Former 91BG crew chief Ira Eakin, far right: 102 Squadron navigator Dickie Mayes and his talisman, "Cottontop," below: An original guard post sign from Bungay (Flixton).

STOP

MILITARY POLICE

STATION

PLEASE IDENTIFY

YOURSELF

ever, it took a little while to get things organized. "Our squadron is running this postal deal like an Easter egg hunt," Keith Newhouse noted. "One day we get the mail at the officers' club, one time at the intelligence officers' room, then the medics have it, and today we pick it up at the MP gate. I hope someone can fall on the solution of one man taking care of it at one place and each man calling for his own. But that's so simple the powers that be will never think of it."

Sergeant Ira Eakin's first assignment, in July 1942, was to a fighter training field at Atcham, recently vacated by the RAF; he next served at Abbotts Ripton, repairing damaged Fortresses and Liberators, and then as a ground crew chief with the 91st Bomb Group based at Bassingbourn, where he compared the amenities unfavorably with those he had earlier enjoyed. "On the main part of the base," he reported, "they had brick barrack blocks, but we were over the road in little Quonset huts with coke burners and double-deck bunks. I never did know this for a fact, but it was rumored that they gave the mess officer a medal for feeding more troops on less chow than anybody in Europe. We got two meals a day. Breakfast was about ten o'clock and consisted usually of marmalade and that sawdust bread and powdered eggs and a cup of hot tea; then about three o'clock we had lamb—well, it started off as lamb chops and two or three days later it would come back as a stew. By the time the stew came around you could smell it a quarter of a mile from the mess hall. I never did care for lamb to begin with.

Man, that was the lousiest chow."

Initially, Keith Newhouse was equally unhappy with the food at Rackheath. "It has gradually improved," he admitted in his journal, "but it surely isn't interesting. We get some whole eggs, and steak once in ten days. The Eighth must have bought the entire U.S. output of orange marmalade, and we get our quota of Spam and powdered eggs. No fresh milk. Coffee has a peculiar green coloring. One new experience is mustard: it is a bland yellow in color, doesn't smell strong, so a liberal first helping is taken. After the flame has cleared away and the smoke stops coming up the windpipe, the victim learns a healthy respect for it. It has no taste, just heat."

Although Spam—the ubiquitous spiced ham—was pallid fare, with little taste of ham and none of spice, most mess hall menus, British and American, tended to include it. Spam fritters were not at all unpleasant, and the cooks at Kimbolton even held a competition in preparing Spam dishes gourmet style.

Either Ken Stone was less critical than his fellow airmen or, as one who was so skinny on enlistment that he had to eat three bananas and drink four pints of water to meet the weight requirement, he needed more sustenance. In general, he approved of the meals at Ridgewell. "The food was good—regular meat and potatoes. The only thing I wouldn't eat was liver. I hated that. But you could go to the Red Cross Aero Club and get a snack and a Coke anytime. Some of the crew drank beer, but I was too young for that. I didn't care about liquor. I got drunk

"I suppose it was the most vital time of my life—the time when I was most alive. One lived at such a concentrated rate. There's never been anything like that time. But it always seemed to be the nicest blokes who didn't come back: the empty places at the breakfast table always belonged to people you had come to like. I don't really want to be reminded about that."

Dickie Mayes, navigator, 102 Sqn.

There is a certain type of doll found in London called the Piccadilly Commando. A typical commando would be named Legion and her middle name would be Host and her last name would be Lots or Many

or Thousands, and she'd probably be wearing a sable cape. When the dark begins to grip the streets, the commandos come out of hiding and head for their respective theaters. The top operators wander along the edges of Hyde Park

right: Bicycles at a Hardwick dining hall, below: A stage show at Framlingham, center: The Aero Club, Flixton, bottom right: 446BG Air Executive Lt. Col. Fred Knorre at Flixton.

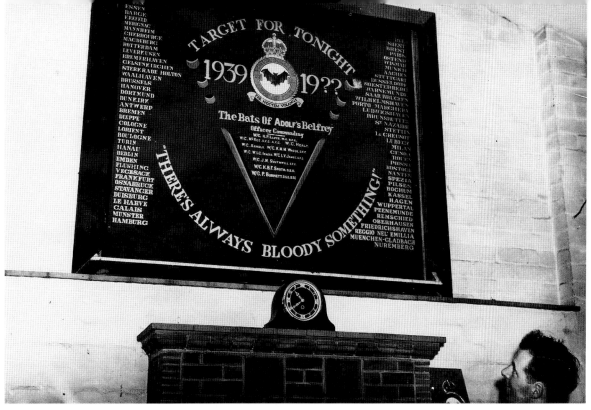

and past the Grosvenor House. There are dark-eyed French girls in the eddies along Bond Street, but most of them are in and around Piccadilly.

—from *Serenade to the Big Bird*, by Bert Stiles.

below: A dance party for the personnel of Base Air Depot 3 at Watton, left: In the officers mess at RAF Bardney, Lincolnshire.

once, on our first leave, but that was the only time I did. We had movies on the base or in town, and dances. I was shy with girls, and I didn't dance. I was a drummer, so I just stood and watched the drummers all the time. I bought a bike and painted it white, and got around on that. We'd bicycle to Halstead and back, and that was good exercise."

Lawrence Drew recalls a minor fracas in his Nissen hut at Grafton Underwood: "The people playing poker had the lights on, and they would play all night. An officer said, 'Come on fellas, have a heart—some guys have got to fly tomorrow.' They just said something back to him and went right on playing, so he took a forty-five from the head of his bed, and walked down the line and shot all those lights out. We had it dark in there after that—for the rest of the night anyway."

Colonel Dale O. Smith found the food at Grafton Underwood less than exciting when he arrived to take command. Seeking an improvement, he sent three mess cooks to study the techniques of hotel chefs in London; next, he used an aircraft starter motor to power a liquidizer for converting powdered eggs and milk into a palatable mixture; finally, he obtained an ice-cream factory, locally abandoned, and set it up on base. Free ice cream for every patron doubled the movie attendance overnight.

It was natural that British airmen, inured to years of rationing, should find little to complain of in the service diet. The quality might leave something to be desired—no mess cook could prepare a meal the way that mother did—but quantities were adequate and more. "I thought it was good," said Tony Partridge of the food at Snaith. "I can't remember having a poor meal. We always had eggs, bacon, and sausage before we went on an op—perhaps that was why we never felt hungry, even on a ten-hour trip."

There were few formal party nights for round-the-clock bomber men, either in RAF messes or Eighth Air Force clubs. Most of the parties occurred spontaneously—somebody's birthday, a promotion, a crew's end of tour, or just because it seemed like a good idea at the time. There would be singing, possibly dancing, probably some beer-drinking races and games—which were quite likely to become increasingly boisterous as the night went on. RAF men traditionally indulged in "High Cockalorum," "Are You There, Moriarty," "Do You Know the Muffin Man," and building human pyramids. American fliers had their own ideas of fun, and since they were far from the comforts of home, these tended to include a feminine element. "English women," said Sidney Rapoport, "were brought in by the truckload. It was a great novelty to them, because of the great expanse of food and beverages—and the gaiety." It was a time for relaxing, for putting footprints on the ceiling, for calling colonels by their first names and maybe for getting just a little drunk. When a USAAF bomb group flew its hundredth mission, the base might celebrate with a three-day stand-down. "I wormed my way into the hundred party of the 91st," said Rapoport. "Everybody let their hair down. I saw Doolittle and

left: The English and their games, overleaf above: The crew library on an 8AF base, overleaf below: A garden party at the Alston home on Lavenham airfield in 1944.

A LITTLE BEHIND on my MAIL But HERE'S WH

☐ BEEN DOIN' K.P.
☐ IN THE GUARD-HOUSE
☐ GOT NO TIME
☐ GOT NO ENVELOPES
☐ GOT NO PAPER

Eaker in a race, trying to push pennies across the floor with their noses. It sure was wild."

Like many young Americans, Calvin A. Swaffer had seen the writing on the wall some months before the Japanese attacked Pearl Harbor. He had enlisted in the Royal Canadian Air Force. He learned to fly, and transferred to the USAAF in 1942. Between October of that year and the following August he flew twenty-five missions as pilot of *The Memphis Blues*, a B-17 of the 303rd Bomb Group, based at Molesworth in Huntingdonshire. "The four officers on our crew slept in one room," he remembered, "and we had no heat in it at all. I slept under seven blankets."

A normal breakfast, in Swaffer's experience, would be of powdered eggs (the fliers called them "square eggs"), and the occasional pancake, but on mission mornings there would be the fresh egg for each man. Other meals consisted principally of Spam, mutton, and Brussels sprouts. "I spent days on end with nothing to do but get up, go to mess, and play games at the officers' club such as Ping-Pong, blackjack, hearts, and checkers, with now and then being called out to fly a combat mission. The club was used by two squadrons. It had a huge fireplace, a games room, and a bar. A whole lot of beer and booze was consumed, especially after a raid."

The officers' club was not a venue highly favored by John B. Thomas, Jr., who flew thirty-five missions as copilot of a B-24 with the 446th at Flixton. "It was usually full

American airmen on leave in London in April 1943.

"Navigation is a problem. We flew some planes in formation to another field, and took two and a half hours to put down at the correct base, although it was only a few miles away. Visibility is so poor it is possible to get lost in your own base pattern. Thank God the radio system is so effective."

Keith Newhouse, pilot, 467BG

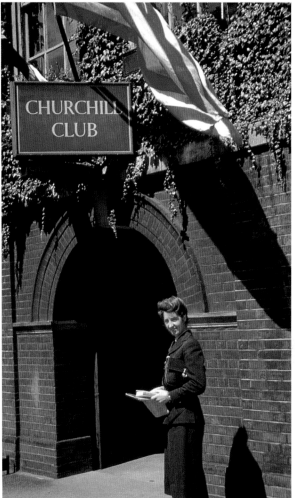

above: A Lancaster at RAF Scampton near Lincoln, above center: Wall art at Shipdham, right: An American Red Cross club near Westminster Abbey.

left: 'Eileen' in faded glory at Knettishall, below left: A pillbox near Metfield, below: The inspection kit of an RAF airman at East Kirkby.

"Our waist gunner met a girl, and they were very much in love. It was a sad parting when he had to leave. I thought maybe he was going to marry her, but he never did."

Ken Stone, ball turret gunner, 381BG

below: English children enjoying GI hospitality at Kimbolton in 1944, right: The ARC Rainbow Corner club in London, below right: Air view of Hardwick, the 93BG base in Norfolk.

90

of base types," he commented, "and we had to fly too much to hang around a lot of permanent poker games and barflies. On a three-day pass, we would take off for Norwich or London."

Calvin Swaffer was another who did not confine his leisure moments to the base. "We got to visit Thrapston, Kettering, and Northampton, and the pubs were great. I learned to drink the warm, dark beer called bitter and play darts. I also got to visit London several times. The most impressive thing was the blackout—the torches people carried around with them, and the 'Underground' they slept in when the German bombers came over. Of course, the British Museum was also impressive, what with the Rosetta stone and the Magna Carta and a lot of other real good stuff. There were tea dances at the Piccadilly Hotel every afternoon, where you would meet officers from all the free countries of western Europe. It was great to meet all those nice people and, above all, the young ladies." Among all his experiences, however, Swaffer maintains that his biggest thrill was having tea at Buckingham Palace with his commanding general as guests of their Majesties the King and Queen of England. (It is pleasant to record that, when the war was over, Swaffer flew on as an airline pilot until he reached the age of sixty. He completed 28,500 flying hours, and never had an accident.)

Depending on the operational requirements, most RAF crews could expect a fair amount of leave: one week in six was the normal allocation, with the prospect of at

above: A Nissen hut at Rattlesden, Suffolk, right: Evidence of 617 (Dambusters) Squadron's stay at RAF Marston Moor in Yorkshire, center above: The Hemswell briefing room, top far right: The Scampton officers' mess, far right: Another of the girls of Shipdham.

least another week at end of tour. Free rail passes were provided for six journeys a year, and Lord Nuffield, the Morris automobile magnate, made funds available for every man to spend a week at a hotel of his choice. For the Eighth Air Force crews, furloughs were usually of shorter duration, with a longer midtour break at a rest and recuperation center—a "flak farm"—located in one of the quieter and less war-torn regions of the English countryside.

Of his stretch at Horsham St. Faith, Charles Bosshardt remembered that he never seemed to get enough sleep. "They would get us up anywhere from one to five A.M. and a high percentage of our missions were scrubbed for weather, and then we flew practice missions or were test hopping or going to ground classes. Any free time we did have we slept as late as we could." Of that winter's weather, he particularly recalled "the worst fog I ever encountered. It froze on the branches and made them look like Christmas trees, sprayed. You could only see about fifty feet in front of you and, being strange to the base, we had to have help from other guys to find the mess hall."

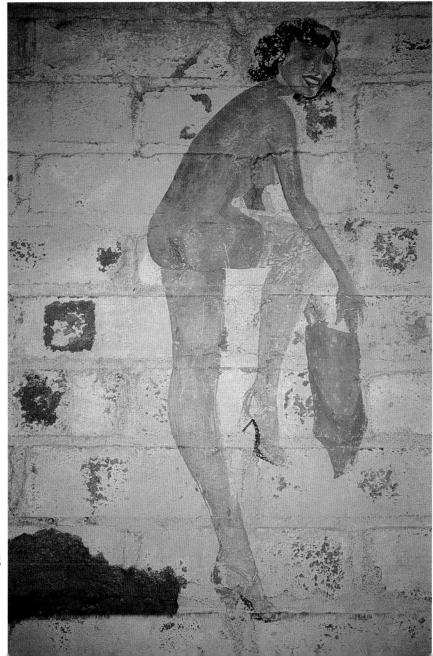

Then I will drink to your good health/ And you shall drink to mine; God never made the grape by stealth, We'll not conceal the wine.

He never made a laughing man/ And meant that man to croak; Then I shall chuckle while I can, And you shall be the joke.

—from "Two Drinking Songs," by A. P. Herbert

94

ON THE NOSE

The bee that hath honey in her mouth hath a sting in her tail.

—from *Euphues*, by John Lyly

She was pretty. She was built. She was American. So she was the past, and a halfway prayer for the future. I could see her in saddle shoes and a knocked-out sweater and skirt. I could see her sucking on a Coke straw, and I could see her all ruffled up after a long ride home in a rumble seat. She was a symbol of something that was always there, in the back of the mind, or out bright in the foreground, a girl with slim brown shoulders, in a sheer white formal with a flower in her hair, dancing through the night.

—from *Serenade to the Big Bird*, by Bert Stiles

left: Examples of 8AF bomber nose art.

ADMIRAL PRUNE

above: The Lancaster *Admiral Prune* is ready to go on a mine laying mission of November 9, 1942, top center: Among the best known and most prolific of the aircraft nose artists of WWII was Tony Starcer of the 91BG. Starcer's illustrations on more than 130 B-17s included *Memphis Belle, Outhouse Mouse, General Ike, Nine O Nine, Dame Satan, Delta Rebel* and *Careful Virgin.* When Tony Starcer designed and applied an illustration to the nose of a bomber, he frequently painted the identical artwork on the A2 jackets of the crew members of that airplane.

"On a seventy-two I never knew exactly what I would do. I would maybe go to London or to Edinburgh in Scotland. Once I went out to Manchester. I was really getting to know England, and loving it . . . a beautiful country."

Sidney Rapoport, radar operator, 94BG

413TH Bombardment Squadron (H)

96TH Heavy Bombardment Group

E SEMPRE L'ORA

SGT. J.L. WHITE
11-24-43

GORINGS NIGHTMARE

far left and below: The art of Sergeant Johnnie White of the 96BG, based at Snetterton Heath, including his working drawing for the B-17 *Goering's Nightmare* and, below, the actual aircraft after a belly landing at Snetterton, left: A 385BG B-17, *Ruby's Raiders,* at Great Ashfield.

Come, lay thy head upon my breast,/ and I will kiss thee into rest.

—from "The Bride of Abydos," by Lord Byron

below: *Milk Wagon,* a 447BG B-17G at the Rattlesden, Suffolk base, far right: B-17F tail art.

A dragon-bearing
Lancaster back from
the Dusseldorf raid of
September 10-11, 1942.

Come to Britain! The rooms are so old/ And so picturesque that you won't mind the cold. The bed's over there and the light's over here; Don't put out your boots if you want them this year;/ The maid has a beard, the cold mutton perspires, But come to Britain and visit the Shires!

Some of you find that Mentone is dull—/ Come over and try a wet Sunday in Hull./ Take luncheon in bed, and get up when you dine, But order your hot-water bottle for nine.

—"COME TO BRITAIN," by A. P. Herbert

When a four-day pass was available we always made a strenuous effort to get into London early enough to find a hotel room. My favorite place was "Prince's Garden," the site of the Eagle Squadron Club of Americans who served with the R.A.F. before the U.S. was drawn into the struggle. It was located far enough away from the beaten path of soldiers on leave that rooms were usually available up to mid-afternoon.

—from *Combat Crew*, by John Comer

"We had a crew chief named Delorenzo, an Italian from New York, very tough. Everything to him was a douchebag, this was a douchebag, the airplane was a douchebag. Everyone around us was naming their planes *Sweet Sue* and stuff like that. We named ours *The Douchebag*. We thought that was a sacred thing—you could name your airplane anything you wanted. But the CO and everybody got on my tail, and made it very difficult for us. We had to change the name. A favorite phrase of the bombardier at that time was a 'dull tool,' that guy's a dull tool, and so on, like saying he was an asshole. So we renamed the airplane *The Dull Tool*, and that's how we went through our tour."

David Parry, pilot, 390BG

far left: A B-17F called *"Meat" Hound,* left above and below: Examples of the art of Philip Brinkman, above, of the 486BG at Sudbury, Suffolk. These illustrations on B-24 Liberators are from the Zodiac series that the artist painted on aircraft of the 834BS in 1944.

AN AMERICAN RAID

BY SERGEANT ROGER A. ARMSTRONG, 91BG, BASSINGBOURN

right: A bomb run is defined by flak bursts and vapor trails over this German target of the 96BG from Snetterton Heath, below: Roger Armstrong on the wing of *The Qualified Quail* at Bassingbourn.

I FELT A TUG on my shoulder, and before I could open my eyes and come out of the wonderful dream I was having, someone tugged again. He put his mouth close to my ear and shone a flashlight in my face. I realized I was not in Sioux Falls, necking with a beautiful brunette at Sherman Park. I was in the 401st Squadron barracks at Bassingbourn, looking at the duty corporal. "Breakfast at 0300," he said, "briefing at 0400, stations at 0515." And he was gone.

I shouldn't have been surprised. The day before, on October 14, 1944, we had dropped "nickels" on Cologne; among them were copies of *The Stars and Stripes* printed in German, with a message to the Luftwaffe from General Doolittle, calling them a bunch of cowards and challenging them to a battle over Cologne the next day. Hilmer Beicker, our flight engineer, was born of German parents in Houston, Texas, and he had read the whole thing out to us over the intercom. We had all pitied the crews who would be going on the next day's mission after an insult like that.

While brushing my teeth, I admired the clean, yellow tiling in our latrine, and I thought how lucky we were to be stationed at a permanent base built by the Royal Air Force in 1938. The latrines were never crowded and we had central heating, so no battles with pot-bellied stoves like we had in basic training.

As I dressed quickly in a suntan shirt and old OD pants, I couldn't help feeling fear, deep inside. I was ashamed to admit that I was afraid, but I found in later years

106

Make hay while the sun shines.

—English proverb

When the truck stopped, and I saw the aircraft we would fly, I was stunned! Of all the planes, we got *Tinker Toy*. No one wanted to fly that plane. It was the jinx ship of the 381st. The tales of her raids read like a book of horror stories. No crew had ever flown her on a routine mission. Invariably it was a life and death struggle to get back. Most people would say there's no such thing as a jinx, but they weren't there to witness the dead men pulled from *Tinker Toy*, or to observe the heavy damage she suffered, raid after raid.

—from *Combat Crew*, by John Comer

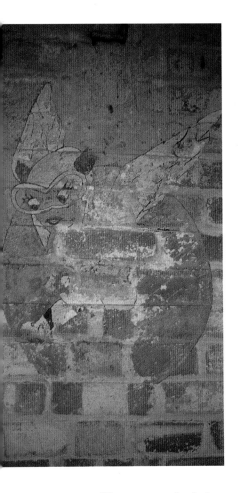

The armorers in their patched faded green, Sweat-stiffened, banded with brass cartridges, Walk to the line; their Fortresses, all tail, Stand wrong and flimsy on their skinny legs, And the crews climb to them clumsily as bears. The head withdraws into its hatch (a boy's), The engines rise to their blind laboring roar,/And the green, made beasts run home to air.

—from "Second Air Force," by Randall Jarrell

that you weren't normal unless you had that feeling. It was really dark when I went outside. I tested the temperature, and put on my fur-collared B-10 jacket. My bike was in a rack outside the door, but the light batteries were dead so I had to steer with one hand, with a flashlight in the other, as I rode to the combat mess hall.

All the combat crews ate at the combat mess so the Air Force could control the types of food we ate. Nothing was fed to us on mission days that would cause gas in the stomach or the intestinal tract, because the gas would expand as your plane climbed to altitude. No one liked the powdered eggs, especially when there were green spots on them. There was a large grill outside the serving line where we could fry eggs to our taste. We purchased our own eggs from the farmer whose backyard was right behind the hardstand of our B-17. When the pilot or the crew chief ran the engines up, the prop wash struck the chicken coops and the feathers really flew. We could never figure out how those hens could lay with all that going on. When the farmer was out of hen eggs, we would buy his duck eggs out of desperation, to avoid those horrible green and yellow powdered eggs.

After breakfast, we drifted over to the briefing building, the only Quonset hut on the base. It was a king-size hut because it had to seat thirty-six or thirty-seven crews. There was a mission map of the British Isles and the Continent on a large board set on the stage, with a curtain hung over it. I sat down with Hilmer and the rest of my crew:

the pilot, John J. Askins, came from Oakland, California; the copilot, Randall H. Archer, from Chester, West Virginia; the navigator, Anthony Delaporta, from Philadelphia, Pennsylvania; the bombardier, Paul W. Collier, from Hamilton, Texas; the waist gunner/armorer, Ralph Azevedo, from Mill Valley, California; the ball turret gunner, Robert N. Webb, Jr., from Dyer, Tennessee; and the tail gunner, Roy E. Loyless, came from Houston, Texas.

I noted that the time was just 0400. Right on cue, one of the Headquarters officers barked, "Tenshut." Colonel Terry walked in at a brisk pace, stepped onto the stage, and said, "At ease, gentlemen." He gave us a pep talk and turned the briefing over to the S-2.

The S-2 walked over to the map, carrying his pool stick, and pulled the curtain up, ever so slowly, as if he savored every moment of the anxiety he was causing in his audience. The red yarn indicated we were going to Cologne, and the reaction was a moan, which gradually crescendoed. The target was the marshaling yards, and we were to disrupt the supplies of armor, artillery, and troops to Aachen, where our soldiers were fighting. There were pieces of red plastic on the map which represented the areas of heavy flak. It bothered us that the S-2 officer would sometimes shift those pieces around, as though he wasn't sure of where the concentrations were. We all knew they were around the large cities; the problem was that no one knew how much mobile flak had been moved into the target area on flatbed train cars.

The weather officer said that the cloud over England was about 19,000 feet thick but not too bad over the Continent. The operations officer gave a time hack so we could set our watches to Greenwich Mean Time, and then we were dismissed. On the way out, we had to pass the three chaplains. Now, I didn't particularly want to be reminded that I might soon meet my Maker, so as we passed I looked the other way. When we got into the fresh air I realized how warm a room could get when the men in there all became concerned about what fate might hold for them that day.

There were other briefings for the pilot, copilot, navigator, bombardier, and me. I reported to the communications building to pick up the codes of the day, the verification codes that were sent when messages were transmitted or received. The communications officer gave me an aluminum briefcase containing the codes, along with log sheets and pencils for recording my messages while on the mission. The codes were printed on rice paper so you could eat them if you were shot down. The officer mentioned that the Germans broke most of our codes within twelve hours. I was also given the colors of the day for the Very lights, which we fired when passing over a convoy or a naval vessel so they wouldn't mistake us for a German plane.

In the equipment room, we collected our Mae Wests, parachutes and harness, oxygen masks, headsets and throat mikes, goggles, gabardine coveralls, heated suits, leather helmets and steel helmets with ear-flaps that covered your headset. There were heated felt inserts to go inside the sheepskin and leather flying boots, and silk gloves to wear inside the heated leather gloves. We stowed the gear in our equipment bags, and then we picked up the escape kits, which contained a silk map, a razor, high-energy candy, a plastic bottle, water purification tablets, and translation sheets in Flemish, Dutch, French, and German.

They had taken photos of us when we arrived at the base, which you were to give to the Resistance if you got shot down, so they could make you an identity document. I never took my photos along (a chief German interrogator told me recently that they could tell your bomb group by the civilian coat you were wearing the day they took your photo). We didn't take the .45-caliber Colt automatics along, either, because S-2 had found the possession of a gun had given the Germans an excuse to shoot you.

It was a five-minute ride in a six-by-six truck from the hangar to the dispersal area where our B-17, *The Qualified Quail*, was parked. We all had our own thoughts and everyone was quiet on the way. It was a gray, depressing morning, and the overcast was down to 100 or 150 feet. The driver stopped in front of our plane. It carried the markings of the triangle "A" on the tail and our squadron letter "K." The wing tips, tail plane, and stabilizer were painted red, which indicated we were in the 1st Combat Wing. The markings helped the group to assemble and then to find our wing. We all looked in the bomb

Vengeance is sweet.

—from *Palace of Pleasure*, by William Painter

Wagner's music is better than it sounds.

—Bill Nye

far left: 487BG wall art surviving at Lavenham in 1992, above: The Army Air Force guide for aerial gunners.

The bombardier was responsible for the bomb load as soon as the aircraft moved away from the hardstand. Those bombs had three safety devices to insure against an accidental explosion: (1) a cotter key had to be removed by hand from the fuse mechanism of each bomb; (2) an arming wire had to pull out of the fuse assembly when the bomb fell from the aircraft; and (3) an impellor had to spin off the fuse assembly from the action of the wind on the drop. As long as any of those safety measures were in place, the bomb was supposed to be inert and no more dangerous than a block of concrete for the same weight. Any

bay to see what kind of bombs we were carrying: if you carried delayed-action bombs, you had to take off anyway, even if the weather changed, and drop them in the North Sea. We had a full load of 250-pound bombs and two clusters of M-17 incendiaries on the top shackles.

I put my heated suit on over my coveralls, and this was a mistake, because as soon as I climbed into the plane to check out the radio room I always got the call of nature. As usual, I found a semisecluded spot to take care of that. At the same time, I could hear Beicker throwing up. He said, "I don't know why, but once I enter the waist door and smell the interior of the plane, I get sick at my stomach." I told him what it did to me and not to worry about it. It was that smell— of oil, gas, canvas flak suits, and ammunition boxes.

In the radio room, I checked the spare chest-type chute pack, the walk-around oxygen bottle, and the four-by-four piece of armor plating the crew chief had found for me. My radios and rack of frequency ranges were all in place, and so was the frequency meter, in case I needed to check the accuracy of what a dial on the receiver read.

John and Randy, with Beicker and the crew chief, checked the exterior and interior of the plane, while the gunners checked their guns and ammunition. When the engines were started, I heard them cough and splutter before they started to run. We put on our headsets and checked the intercom, and then John ran the engines up while the ground crew stood by with fire extinguishers.

The plane vibrated and became very noisy. I heard the sound of the brakes being released as John moved onto the taxiway and fell in behind the ship we were to follow in the line for takeoff. I turned on my radios and the IFF. I would monitor the Division frequency during the mission; the IFF would send a continuous code while we were over friendly territory so the coastal defenses wouldn't shoot at us.

The lead squadron took off at 0600, and by 0622 all twelve were airborne. John turned onto the runway and ran the engines while he held the brakes on. The plane kind of jerked into a rolling start as he released them. Runway 25 was 6,000 feet long, but it seemed he was never going to lift that heavy load off as we gathered speed. Then the plane broke loose from the pull of gravity and we were airborne. I noticed I had held myself stiff while we were moving down that runway, but now I relaxed. Watching out of the radio room window by my desk, I saw we were higher than the village church steeple, then suddenly we were in the overcast and flying blind.

John had to fly at a given speed and rate of climb for so many minutes, then turn right, still climbing, and turn again so we were making one big square around the Bassingbourn Buncher beacon. It was quite nerve-racking in the overcast. It was so thick, I could barely see the left wing tip. A voice on the intercom said, "Submarine at nine o'clock level." It was Azevedo, the right waist gunner. No one answered. The plane bounced around and we knew it was from

110

B-17s of the 381BG based at Ridgewell in Essex, in the basic 3-ship combat element.

the prop wash of another B-17 out there somewhere.

Randy's voice came over the intercom: "Copilot to crew, we are passing through 10,000 feet, so oxygen masks on, please." A few minutes later he said, "Oxygen check," and we answered to our names from tail to nose: "Loyless okay," "Azevedo okay," "Webb okay," and finally "Collier okay."

We broke out of the overcast for a few minutes, and saw twenty or thirty B-17s around us. The third squadron from the 91st was just below us. Then, we were climbing back into the cloud, still making squares over the base Buncher. Finally it began to look a little lighter and we popped out of the

mess. We were to fly high squadron of the group, and the group was to lead the 1st Combat Wing, with one wing ahead of us. Collier saw the lead squadron forming up and we located our element leader of the high squadron. It was still hazy, but with just sufficient visibility to get the group formed, and we set course for Clacton at 20,000 feet. The 381st and 398th Bomb Groups had taken off after us, and our group leader did a series of "S" turns to let them catch up and form the combat wing.

We left Clacton two minutes early at an altitude of 21,000 feet. The winds over the Channel were greater than briefed, and John told Tony, the navigator, that the whole wing

of those devices would restrict the striker pin from igniting the explosion at the moment of impact with the ground.

—from *Combat Crew*, by John Comer

Airmen often believed they would not return from a mission if they made their beds before leaving (an unmade bed indicated that its owner would return to sleep there again).

"There isn't anybody that wants to get killed. You'd go into the briefing room and you'd get the weather officer, intelligence, flak positions, and so forth. They'd pull the curtain back and you'd see this line going to the target and you'd think, 'Oh, boy, I'm not going on this, this'll kill me.' And then you'd say, 'What I'll do is I'll wait a while and then I'll go on sick call and get out of it.' Then you'd go down to the airplane and you'd figure, 'Well, I'll go on sick call later.' And then you'd see everybody get in their planes and you'd know they were just as frightened as you were, and you'd think, 'What

was doing another "S" turn because we were catching up on the wing ahead of us. We were at 27,000 feet when we arrived at point 2 on the route to Cologne, still two minutes early but with everyone spaced at normal intervals. Over the bomber channel, I heard the weather ship, *Buckeye Blue,* report that the route weather was good but that contrails were forming at the bombers' altitude. Then *Buckeye Red* said that Cologne was overcast and that the PFF ships would be needed to locate and zero in on the target with radar.

Out over the Channel, just before we reached the Continent, the gunners had test-fired their guns. They had charged their guns before we reached high altitude, because the barrel shrank at low temperature, and if you didn't have a shell in it, the gun probably wouldn't fire.

As we flew toward Cologne, Tony called John and said: "We're running parallel to the front lines, that's why we can see flak up ahead." I thought, why aren't we flying on the Allied side, instead of over the German lines? Meantime, I was copying a message for the wing commander in the lead ship from the 1st Air Division. There were about a dozen German ground operators jamming the frequency, but Division was sending the Morse on a modulated tone that sounded like a big truck horn honking. You soon got used to that tone, and the jamming didn't really bother you.

We had put our flak suits on as we entered German territory, and I snapped the chest pack on the right ring of my harness. It left an area vulnerable, but I felt the chute would absorb low-velocity flak or even a bullet fired at long range. Suddenly the plane rose and fell four or five times. There was flak below us, not doing any damage but it was worrying me. I concentrated on copying some of the German code, because the busier you were the less you thought about getting hit, but they were just holding their keys down or tapping out a series of v's. I lost interest and got back to trying to get rid of the ache in my chest, thinking about the curtains of flak we would be going through at Cologne.

The wing commander started a series of "S" turns to throw the German gunners off, and John told us what was happening. We all felt John was the best pilot in the group, and he was also a good communicator. He always advised us what was going on. We in turn watched out from our positions and told him if we noticed any mechanical or structural problem with the plane.

I listened in on the group voice channel and heard the pilot of the lead PFF ship in the low squadron say, "We have lost our bombing radar." The lead command ship said, "Drop on our smoke bombs at the target."

We were getting both tracking flak and box barrage flak as we flew past Cologne to the south and picked up our IP, where we started our run in to the target. The plane was really bouncing up and down, and I moved my piece of armor plating across the radio room to the chaff chute. We were carrying seven cartons of chaff bundles, which were held together by paper strips until they were pushed though the chute and hit the slipstream. Our group would create thousands of false blips on the enemy's radar screens to help the groups behind us, the way the group ahead was helping us. On the right side of the ship, I built up a flak shack of chaff cartons on my armor plating. Webb was too large to wear his flak helmet in the

the hell, I'll go about a hundred miles and find something wrong with the airplane.' But they had this tradition that an Eighth Air Force sortie never turned back from the target. So in the end you didn't dare turn back."

Ray Wild, pilot, 92BG

When your neighbor's house is afire your own property is at stake.

—Horace

above: At Kimbolton, reflying the mission. left: *The Worry Bird*, at Flixton after a mission.

ball turret, so he loaned it to me. I pulled my own helmet down over my eyes, placed Webb's over my reproductive organs, and started throwing chaff.

Suddenly the radio room lit up bright red, and the plexiglass roof window blew inward in a thousand pieces with a number of shell fragments. Then another shell exploded just above the nose. We went into a dive, leveled out, and eased back into the formation. What had happened was that a piece of flak had come through the windshield and struck John on the right shoulder of his flak suit, turning him in a clockwise direction and making him chop all four engines with his right hand, which was holding the throttles. Randy had pushed the throttles forward and flown us back into position.

right: Post-mission whiskey at a 93BG interrogation, far right: A safe return to Hardwick.

Hilmer Beicker came out of the top turret and saw John struggling to turn himself forward. His seat belt was so tight he was having a tough time, so Beicker went to help him. At that moment, Randy reached for his flak helmet and was just putting it on when another piece of flak came through the window and struck him on the head. Beicker stopped him from falling on the yoke, and grabbed the first-aid kit. Randy came to and shook his head as Beicker was wiping the blood out of his eyes. It turned out that the flak had only grazed his forehead.

Beicker took a look at the instruments, looked around the flight deck, and went back to the top turret. There was a hole in the plexiglass and a chunk out of the housing; otherwise the turret was in good shape.

I was just throwing a bundle of chaff out when another close burst, which I heard, sent three pieces through the skin of the plane four or five inches from my head. If I had been reaching for another bundle, my head would have taken all three fragments. The holes peeled outward, so the fragments had come right through the ship. I looked around: the right side of my liaison set had a hole the size of your fist in it.

Another burst hit us, and a piece of flak struck my left glove, ripping the leather open from my wrist to the end of my thumb. I felt the blood get warm on my hand, and visualized the thumb—shot off inside the glove. I didn't want to take the glove off, but I knew I had to because of the bleeding. I was relieved when I saw that the thumb was still attached to my hand. I dumped some sulfa

114

out of the first-aid kit on two cuts and put a bandage on. This had kind of held my attention, and I realized that John had been calling on the intercom: "Pilot to radio, pilot to radio . . ."

I answered: "Radio to pilot."

"Pilot to radio—Azevedo is down in the waist. See what's wrong."

I grabbed my walk-around oxygen bottle and took off for the waist. Azevedo was lying on his back. I saw him blink, so I knew he was alive. When I squatted down beside him, it was obvious he had been hit in the right thigh. Having checked that his mask was securely connected to the right waist oxygen supply, I disconnected my walk-around bottle and plugged into the left waist hose. I took my Boy Scout knife and cut the leg of

At sixteen thousand I took off my helmet. There was a puddle of drool in my oxygen mask. I rubbed my face but it felt like a piece of fish. The candy bar tasted wonderful.

—from *Serenade to the Big Bird*, by Bert Stiles.

We all had flak on our minds. The terrible thing was the enforced passivity. You could strike back against fighters, and under attack from them we shouted a lot on the interphone to work together in our common defense. With flak we just had to sit there and fly through it and hope they'd miss. Before the actual bombing run we took evasive action with turns of ten degrees or so every twenty or thirty seconds; it had all been laid out in the briefing. But on the run we had to fly straight as a pool cue for ninety seconds, and that was when I felt most helpless. There we sat, strapped down with safety belts, so a near miss wouldn't knock us out of our seats, and waited.

—from *The War Lover,* by John Hersey

I Never Have Enough

RAZOR BLADES ☐

SHAVING CREAM ☐

CIGARETTES .. ☐

CANDY .. ☐

COOKIES . ☐

FRUIT... ☐

"Keep 'em Flying!"

his pants open. The hole was the size of a silver dollar. It was bleeding but not pumping blood, so I assumed the fragment had missed the femoral artery.

When I took my gloves off, my fingers stiffened up so they wouldn't function properly. I had to keep putting the gloves on to warm up. It got so bad I called the pilot and told him I needed help. By this time I was feeling a little drunk and I kind of plopped down beside Azevedo on my behind. He kept pointing at the ceiling, and I looked up and saw that the oxygen line I was plugged into had been sliced in two. I thought, although the flak had eased off, they were still trying to get me, one way or another. I plugged back into the walk-around bottle and after a few deep breaths of pure oxygen I felt normal. It wasn't as good as feeling half-drunk.

Beicker arrived to help, and between the two of us we got a pressure bandage on Azevedo's wound, but the temperature at our altitude did more to stop the bleeding. The copilot called for an oxygen check, and the first on his list didn't answer, so I crawled on back to the tail, lugging the walk-around bottle. I got to Loyless on my hands and knees. His eyes were as big as saucers and he was holding the cord to his mike, which a piece of flak had cut in two, three or four inches from his throat. I plugged into his jack box and told Randy what had happened.

Back at the waist, Beicker had found that the piece of flak had come out at the back of Azevedo's thigh. We started all over

stopping the blood at that point and putting sulfa on the wound. Then we bandaged him up and put a couple of blankets round his legs. To talk to Beicker I had to take my mask off, yell in his ear, and put the mask back on quick. I yelled, "Maybe we should give him a shot of morphine—he could be going into shock."

Beicker held his cupped hand behind my ear: "I think we should. You give it to him."

My medical knowledge was confined to what I had picked up in the Boy Scouts, *Reader's Digest,* and a Red Cross class at Creighton University in the Aviation Cadet program. I yelled back, "I've never given a shot before. Maybe you should do it: you know all about engines and stuff like that."

Beicker's eyes looked kind of funny. "So what? You know all about radios. And you showed me a Red Cross card one time where it said you had qualified for first aid."

Azevedo was lying there and he could hear my side of the conversation in his headset. He kept trying to get our attention, and finally he said, "You guys aren't giving me any dope."

I said, "Look, Azzie, you haven't got much say in this matter."

He said, "Neither one of you guys knows anything about medicine. And when we got our shots at Sioux City, Beicker fainted when the first needle went into his arm."

That was true; they gave him three more shots while he was on the floor. Anyway, I was about to lose my voice from yell-

116

ing. I took the morphine out of the first-aid kit. It looked like a small tube of toothpaste with a needle in the end. I warmed it under my heated suit and aimed the needle at the muscle a few inches from the front hole in his thigh. At first I pushed real easy and it didn't go in. I looked up at Beicker. He looked away. I shoved hard and it slid into the thigh. I squeezed the tube, and in a few minutes Azevedo had drifted off to sleep.

I looked out of the window and saw we were still in flak. The plane shook and a burst over the nose knocked the bombardier off his seat. Later, I saw the dent in his helmet, and a lump on his head to match. He crawled back to the bombsight and I heard him say, "Bomb bay doors are opening, follow the PDI." That was the pilot direction indicator on the instrument panel.

The group's bombs were dropped from 27,000 feet at 0928. The clouds had cleared and we were able to see our bombs striking the marshaling yards. John had feathered the numbers one and three engines while we were working on Azevedo. Other planes near us also had engines feathered. John got number one engine started again and we were able to stay with the formation. Several bombers from the lead and low squadrons were straggling behind. On the fighter channel, I heard the lead ship ask for "little friends" to assist the damaged planes.

There was cloud at our altitude when we reached the Channel, and the group let down to get under it. This helped the stragglers to keep up with the formation. The fighter protection was excellent. At 1143 we

crossed the English coast at Clacton, and the wing broke up with each group heading back to its own base, pretty well strung out and flying loose.

I went back every ten minutes to see if Azevedo was okay. I took his pulse to see if maybe he had died, but his heart was beating and his skin was warm. I took his mask off when we were at low altitude. John called me to the flight deck as we approached Bassingbourn, and asked me to load the Very pistol with red/red flares to show he had injuries aboard. Looking out through the broken window I saw a number of planes also flying flares. On the final approach, the tail and ball gunners took their positions in the radio room, and the navigator and bombardier came out of the nose.

The ambulances were lined up on the left of runway 25. As we touched down, one raced along the grass beside the runway, and when we turned off and stopped near the tower the medics were ready to come aboard and remove Azevedo. Instead of taking him to the base hospital they took him to Wimpole Hall, which was set up to treat the more serious injuries. I was kind of glad they took him there. It had been the home of Rudyard Kipling, who was a favorite in my family. My father used to quote Kipling's poems in his sermons at Sioux Falls.

We left *The Qualified Quail* by the tower with a number of other badly damaged B-17s, and a truck took us to the interrogation building. We were escorted to a table where the S-2 officer poured double shots of scotch into coffee cups. He wanted to

117

For the cause that lacks
assistance, The wrong
that needs resistance,
For the future in the
distance,/ And the good
that I can do.

—from "What I Live
For" by George
Linnaeus Banks

overleaf: Roger A.
Armstrong, below: Belly
landing at Bassingbourn,
top left: A 390BG crew is
safely home from a raid,
top right: Interrogation at
Framlingham, below right:
At Great Ashfield after the
raid of October 9, 1943.

know what we all saw on the mission and asked about our injuries.

Randy was sitting next to me; he had pulled up his jacket sleeve and was pushing at something just under the skin of his arm. It was a metal splinter, about four inches long. He had worked it almost out when the S-2 asked what he was doing. Randy said, "I felt my arm itch. I just found a piece of flak in it." He pulled it out all the way and put it in his pocket. The S-2 saw the nicks on his forehead and asked if he wanted to see the flight surgeon. Randy said no, he had a date. I did too. I said I had treated my cut hand in the plane. John didn't mention the bruise on his shoulder; he told me later it was sore for three weeks.

After interrogation we took a look at *The Qualified Quail.* After finding two hundred holes we got tired of counting. John, Beicker, and the crew chief were looking at something under the right wing. As I walked up, John said, "Our main spar was almost shot in two. If I had known about it, I wouldn't have banked so steep, and I would have taken it easier coming in for landing." It turned out that of thirty-six B-17s of the 91st Bomb Group, sixteen sustained minor damage and twenty had major damage.

We had an excellent lunch of steak and potatoes, with ice cream for dessert. I took a shower and went into Royston where I met my date. We did some pub-crawling, and next morning I slept in as we didn't fly a mission. Two days later, they sent us back to Cologne.

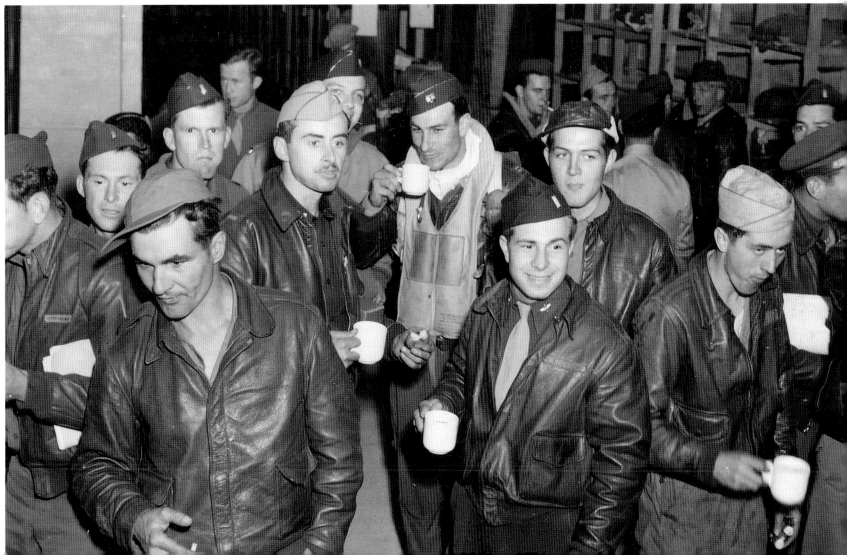

DINGHY, DINGHY, PREPARE TO DITCH!

JUST HOW MANY WARPLANES ditched in the waters between England and Europe while returning from their missions will never be accurately known, but of the airmen who were reported to have ditched, or whose last distress messages were received by radio, it is certain that the majority survived. This was largely due to the efforts of the Air-Sea Rescue Service, jointly controlled by the RAF and the Royal Navy, and tasked with saving airmen of the Allied forces (and sometimes of the Luftwaffe) from the perils of the sea.

The first sea rescue of an American bomber crew in World War II was effected on October 2, 1942, after the Eighth's "first real brawl" over Lille. Two damaged B-17s had gone down in the English Channel, and what follows is the story of the one whose crew was saved. "The fun began," the pilot stated, "as we started home. We got plenty of flak, and we were under attack from fighters. A Focke-Wulf 190 winged us with a cannon shell, and the outer starboard engine started smoking quite badly. The generators were

"Everybody had a designated position to go to before you hit the water. The pilot and the copilot let their seats back all the way, and that ain't the easiest place to try to gauge distance when you put an airplane down. The rest of the crew were behind the bomb bay with their backs against the bulkhead. They drew their knees up and the guys in front of them leaned against their knees. We went through the drill once a month, in case we ever had to ditch."

Robert White, pilot, 390BG

knocked out and the intercom went dead."

There was probably more damage than the crew were aware of, for the aircraft lost altitude at fifteen hundred feet a minute. As every wartime airman knew, the Channel was the shortest stretch of water in the world on the outbound route, and the longest coming back. The pilot decided that, on this occasion, it was going to be too long. It so happened that his crew had practiced ditching drills the day before the mission, but

then they had been able to use the intercom; now, when it mattered, communication had to be by word of mouth.

Five thousand feet above the water, the pilot handed over to the copilot and went aft. To lighten the aircraft, he had the waist guns jettisoned, and instructed the gunners to assemble in the radio compartment; the navigator and the bombardier were told to join them from the nose. "Then I went back to the controls," said the pilot, "and got ready

Airmen who had survived ditchings said that contact with the water was like driving into a brick wall at forty miles an hour. You stood an excellent chance of being knocked unconscious by the impact—and it was a bad time to be unconscious because as soon as the aircraft stopped smashing and splashing through the water it was desirable to get out. Hurriedly.

—from *Bomb Run*, by Spencer Dunmore

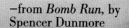
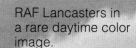

RAF Lancasters in a rare daytime color image.

Dear Boys of the R.A.F., I have just seen that the R.A.F. flyers have a life-saving jacket they call a "Mae West," because it bulges in all the "right places." Well, I consider it a swell honour to have such great guys wrapped up in you, know what I mean? Yes, it's kind of a nice thought to be flying all over with brave men . . . even if I'm only there by proxy in the form of a life-saving jacket, or a life-saving jacket in my form. I always thought that the best way to hold a man was in your arms—but I guess when you're up in the air a plane is safer. You've got to keep everything under control. Yeah, the jacket idea is all right, and I can't imagine anything better than to bring you boys of the R.A.F. soft and happy landings. But what I'd like to know about that life-saving jacket is—has it got dangerous curves and soft shapely shoulders? / You've heard of Helen of Troy, the dame with the face that launched a thousand ships . . . why not a shape that will stop thousands of tanks? If I do get in the dictionary—where you say you want to put me—how will they describe me? As a warm and clinging life-saving garment worn by aviators? Or an aviator's jacket that supplies the woman's touch while the boys are flying around nights? How would you

to ditch the ship. We removed our parachutes and adjusted our Mae Wests. The water looked cold, and it also looked hard."

There had never been such a thing as a practice ditching. You could rehearse the drill for taking up position in the aircraft, bracing for the impact, and finding the cables that released the dinghies; in the local swimming pools, you could practice inflating the Mae West, handling the dinghy, and trying to climb aboard; but the only time a pilot set an airplane down on water was when there was nothing else to do. As to how it should be done, instructions in the manuals tended to be sparse. They suggested it was best to lower a little flap and touch down with the airplane in a level attitude; there was a further, if unwritten, school of thought that advocated ditching along the swell rather than across it; but no pilot could be blamed, in the stresses of the moment, if he failed to bear all those maxims in his mind. The Flying Fortress pilot did his best.

"We laid her down," he said, "in a belly landing as slowly as we could, with the tail well down. There were waves, and I had heard that when you hit a wave the effect is very much like flying into a stone wall. It was. We hit so hard that it threw the crew all over the ship."

Two men were knocked unconscious, and the others were momentarily dazed. Coming to their senses, they tried to launch the dinghies, of which two had been so damaged as to be unseaworthy; the third could be only partially inflated. "Then came another problem," the pilot continued. "When

the men started dropping into the water, they realized that the winter equipment some of them were wearing was too heavy for their Mae Wests to support. Splashing around in the icy water, those in lighter clothing managed to hold the others up while they got out of their leather jackets, trousers, and flying boots, and struggled into their life preservers again. I saw the copilot float out of a window and drift under the wing. I swam after him and managed to grab him and drag him to the dinghy. Then the navigator's log floated past, so I retrieved that. About then everything seemed perfectly logical. I was doing some careful reasoning. The trouble was that I didn't always get the right answer."

The airplane sank in approximately a minute and a half. Some of the crewmen climbed into the dinghy while some stayed in the water, holding to the sides. One of the gunners, believing that the dinghy would not support another man, was determined to sacrifice himself: "He'd go down, come up spitting water, and then go down again; he kept on trying to make us let him go. It took a direct order to make him behave.

"Then came the worst part," the pilot reported, "waiting for help to get there and wondering if any help was going to come. What we didn't know was that we were as good as rescued already. Before our ship hit the water the machinery of HM Air-Sea Rescue Service had started to roll. The lead plane in our Spitfire escort had told them that we were going down and given them our approximate location. We were in the water only thirty-five minutes, and during that time one of the RAF Spits was circling to indicate our position."

The rescue boat appeared behind a foaming bow wave and came alongside. The crew seemed unfriendly, scowling down into the dinghy. Then one of the airmen called a greeting, and the sailors' manner changed. "Hell, they're Yanks!" someone shouted. "Hold on, maties! We'll have you out of there in half a mo'."

The pilot soon discovered why the sailors' attitude had been short of warmth: "They thought we were Germans because of the powder-blue color of the electrically heated suits a couple of the gunners wore. It seems they couldn't work up any enthusiasm about picking Germans up. Our rescue constituted a special occasion for them, because the boat crews had organized a pool to be won by the first to pick up some Americans."

Despite the minor hiccups, that first Fortress rescue was a model operation. But it had advantages denied to many others: an October afternoon in the English Channel was a different proposition from a midwinter night in the width of the North Sea. Those Fortress crewmen, for example, clinging to the dinghy, would not have been alive when the rescue boat arrived had they ditched further north at a later time of year.

Between eleven o'clock and midnight on Wednesday, January 5, 1944, a force of 348 Lancasters set out from their bases to attack the port of Stettin, at the point where the river Oder joins the Baltic Sea. As the crews made their bomb runs, the sparkle of gunfire, the glow of marker flares, the flames of incendiaries, and the prodigious flash of "cookies" were mirrored by the snow and reflected from the river. Careless of the flak, the black-crossed german night fighters fired streams of tracer as they swept into the bomber stream. It was a spectacle not to be forgotten.

When the returning bombers were still two hundred miles from the English coast, the awakening sun behind them seemed to touch the clouds with gold. The Merlin engines droned; the crews were silent at their posts. They were looking forward to breakfast and to bed. Two hours behind the main stream and 10,000 feet below it, Australian Noel Belford's crew in T-Tommy 2 from 12 Squadron's base in Lincolnshire were less favorably placed. They, like the rest, had bombed the center of the markers just before four o'clock in the morning, and turned for home. It was some hours later, when the mid-upper gunner asked how it could be that the polestar lay astern if they were flying west, that their predicament emerged.

Navigator Arthur Lee then checked the pilot's repeater of the master compass and realized the truth: the gyro had gradually precessed, the way that gyros will, and the pilot had followed it, the way that pilots will. Tommy 2 had not been flying home: she had been flying in the arc of an enormous circle. After an hour or two, the engineer announced that, if they were careful, the fuel might last for another thirty minutes, give or take ten minutes either way. At eight o'clock

in the morning, when the gee signals started to come through, Lee established where they were. They were over the islands of the Frisians: where they should have been was on the ground at Wickenby.

Shortly before ten o'clock, when his colleagues back in England were falling into bed, Belford determined to ditch Tommy 2 while he still had engine power for control. He made the same decision about the approach as the Fortress pilot had. "Noel made several dummy runs," said Lee, "and decided to land across the troughs, using the wave crests to slow the aircraft down. I took a final gee fix, wrote the coordinates on a scrap of paper, and put it in the capsule on the carrier pigeon's leg. The wireless operator clamped his key down. I stuffed the Very pistol and cartridges in my battle-dress blouse. The engineer stayed with the pilot to help with the ditching, while the rest of us scrambled over the main spar and squatted down with our hands clasped behind our heads, ready for the impact.

"We hit the water with an almighty crash, the sea poured in through the open hatches, and we thought we were going down, but the inrush was caused by waves breaking over us. The aircraft was bobbing on the surface, and we made an orderly exit onto the wing. The dinghy inflated automatically and burst out of its housing. Unfortunately, we failed to secure it to the aircraft, and it began to drift away. We leaped into the sea and caught it as it passed the tail plane. We watched the last minutes of Tommy 2 as she went down some fifty yards away."

124

So they stayed, drenched in spray, rocking in the swell, telling each other that someone, somewhere, must have heard their signals and would surely come to find them. Two hours later, it seemed that their hopes would be fulfilled. They heard the sound of engines and, looking to the west, saw a Lockheed Hudson flying steadily toward them. The aircraft circled, released a smoke float to find the wind direction, and dropped a Lindholme dinghy—a navigable lifeboat—a hundred yards away. Belford's crew knew that the vessel was equipped with clothing, food, and blankets, but although they paddled after it until they were exhausted, it drifted away from them, farther and farther, and disappeared from sight. The Hudson navigator had misread the wind.

The only comfort for Belford and his men was that their position was obviously known and, sure enough, in midafternoon, a flight of Spitfires gave them an impromptu low-level air display. Then the fighter pilots waved, waggled their wings, and flew away. As night fell on the North Sea, some instinct told the crew that they must not fall asleep, and so they sang. None of them was an overtly religious man, but, by mutual consent, they constantly chorused "Eternal Father, Strong to Save." "And ever since," Lee recorded, "that hymn has deeply moved me. I see the six young faces in the bobbing dinghy, trying to stay alive."

Shortly before midnight they heard another aircraft, and fired a Very light. Things happened quickly after that: a series of flares, the beam of a searchlight, and a bullhorn calling, "Stay where you are until I come alongside."

"Two hefty matelots grasped our arms," Lee recounted, "and, as the dinghy rose on the swell, hauled us aboard one by one. We were rushed belowdecks, dried, wrapped in blankets, and given hot soup. I climbed into a bunk and was asleep within seconds. It was fifteen hours since we ditched."

Friday, January 7, was a better day for Belford's crew. It was revealed they had been saved, not as they expected by the RAF, who had been discouraged by the heavy seas, but by a Royal Navy crew who had set out on many such a mission only to find a vacant dinghy or an empty sea. Rescuers and rescued were delighted with each other; autographs and items of equipment were happily exchanged; cigarettes were smoked and rum was swallowed in mutual esteem. The captain of the launch congratulated Belford on his selection of a ditching area—the outer edge of a minefield. At noon, they entered Yarmouth harbor with all flags flying and the launch's bullhorn repeatedly bellowing, "We've got seven." The boats in the estuary responded with a chorus of siren shrieks.

Initially, the news of the crew's survival was warmly received by their comrades at Wickenby; successful ditchings in the Lancaster were extremely rare. They were less pleased when, following an unguarded statement by one of Belford's crew that, unlike the Fortress men, he had never done a dinghy drill, the CO ordered everyone to practice the procedure until they could perform it in their sleep.

took up the slack with a steady stream of fire to keep the swarming fighters at bay. Another shell exploded, wounding Sergeant Vosler in the chest and face. He kept firing his gun. Surviving its ordeal over the North Sea, the bomber was forced to ditch off Cromer, England. Although blinded by metal fragments, Sergeant Vosler was able to repair the damaged radio and send distress signals between periods of unconsciousness. After the ditching, he escaped the plane and kept the wounded tail gunner afloat until both men were pulled into a dinghy. Sergeant Vosler was discharged in October 1944 after prolonged hospital treatment.

—from the obituary of Forrest L. Vosler, *Air Force* magazine, April 1992.

above left: The German air force bringing bombs to England via Dornier Do-17 twin-engined "Flying Pencils." Many of the Do-17 crews were to experience English hospitality, or the killing temperatures of the North Sea. below left: Battle damage, fuel shortages and other woes frequently caused aircraft of the Allied air forces to ditch in North Sea or Channel waters.

COUNTRY FOLK

There was an old hen And she had a wooden leg, And every damned morning She laid another egg; She was the best damned chicken On the whole damned farm−/ And another little drink Wouldn't do us any harm.

−American folk song

She walks in beauty like the night/ Of cloudless climes and starry skies; And all that's best of dark and bright/ Meet in her aspect and her eyes: Thus mellowed to that tender light/ Which Heaven to gaudy day denies.

−from "She Walks in Beauty," by Lord Byron

English evacuee kids being entertained by American Red Cross personnel at the Grafton Underwood home of the 384BG.

THE ARRIVAL IN EAST ANGLIA of the U.S. Eighth Army Air Force made a major impact on local hearts and minds. In succession through the centuries, the native people's ancestors had suffered invasion by the Roman legions, the Scandinavian pirates, and the Norman French; they had endured occupation for a century or two, and, eventually, their visitors had gone. And since their warships and their weather had repulsed the Spanish galleons, no invader had approached their shores. In 1940, when the German armies stood poised just across the Channel, these same people had been prepared to meet them in the fields and villages with pitchforks and ploughshares. Thanks to their airmen, there had been no need. Two years later, they faced an invasion from which the only threat was to their innate insularity and habit of reserve.

The incomers were benign but unfamiliar; they were open-handed and gregarious; they had few inhibitions. They said "Hi" and smiled at people who had not smiled for quite a while. They were obviously affluent, compared with British servicemen, and far better dressed. They were never short of Lucky Strikes, Chesterfields, or Camels; they seemed to have instant access to perfume and nylon stockings; they tended to chew gum and to perform a strange caper called the jitterbug; they preferred cold beer and warm accommodation, neither of which was readily available. They drawled like Gary Cooper or rapped their words out like James Cagney; they cut their food up with a knife and ate it with a fork. Even so, they were

below: The 385BG's Jim Dacey, and friends, right: A local lad in Royston, 1944.

accepted as potent allies, and most people thought of them as friends. Only the crabbier, and perhaps the envious, complained that they were "overpaid, oversexed, and over here." (One of those Yanks was later to riposte that the Brits were underpaid, undersexed, and under Eisenhower.)

John Skilleter, a youthful evacuee from London, was billeted in Woodbridge, Suffolk, when the Eighth Air Force arrived. "If there was no flying," he wrote, "the Yanks would hit the town. Usually they came in jeeps and six-by-six trucks but more often on bicycles, caps on the backs of their heads, slacks rolled up below the knee and sporting fancy cowboy boots. They came in crews—young officers side by side with weathered non-coms and non-shaving boy gunners, all keen to find a pub that was not 'officers only,' as many were. There were fights over local girls, fights with British serviceman, and fights between drunken buddies for the hell of it. We couldn't understand them, but the old soldiers among us did. The clues were out there in the craters made by crashed aircraft in the Suffolk mud."

There was one trait in particular which endeared the Americans to those who were aware of it, and that was their attitude to kids. Ira Eakin gave an instance of the sort of thing that happened wherever they were based: "When we was on that fighter base we adopted a little blond-headed girl. Her parents got killed and Captain Tracy found out about it some way. The cutest little blond-headed girl you ever saw. She was just an angel. Tracy would call down at this orphan-

age that had her and they'd let her come up to the base for the weekend. We had Red Cross women on the base that looked after her at night. Guys were kicking in around a pound and ol' Tracy come in and he said, 'Hell, you can do better than that. I gave sixty pounds and I want at least ten from you cats.' And we did, and we got it all fixed up and sent her back to the States. Often wondered whatever happened to her."

"We would land in the afternoon," said tail gunner Paul Sink, "and there was a road around the base to kind of separate us from the surrounding countryside. And these little boys, ten, eleven, twelve years old, they'd be standing there, peering through the hedgerows, watching us get out of the airplanes. We'd have the heavy flying kit, flak jackets, oxygen masks hanging from our helmets. I suppose we did look pretty strange."

Reactions varied among the female population: some declared roundly that they didn't care for Yanks; others remained true to their sweethearts in the forces—true in their fashion, anyway; many had the time of their young lives whenever the USAAF came to town or threw a party on the base. Often, a casual acquaintanceship blossomed into romance, sometimes into a marital commitment. Eakin's courtship of a pretty English nurse did not go quite so far: "I met her shortly after I went over there and I dated her most of the time. We almost got married, but it ended up we didn't. She said my folks would think she'd married me just to come to the United States. I asked her if she felt that way about it and she said, 'I would like to go to the United States but I wouldn't marry anybody just to go there.' I found 'em real good, just real understanding. Sure, they liked to go out and have a good time, dance and all this, and a few other things, but not that big a difference."

"I went with this girl Jill," said bombardier Larry Bird. "She was a dancer, about eighteen or nineteen years of age, and very independent. We used to go out in London and get caught in the air raids. We spent nights in the subway, and got home in the morning. Her parents didn't mind. They were so doggone nice, I'll never forget them. They were people of some standing. They had a car, and not everyone in England had a car in those days. It was up on blocks in the yard, on account of no gasoline. Most people depended on the bicycle. If you had a bicycle, you had transportation."

Roger W. Armstrong, of the 91st Bomb Group, remembered this of Bassingbourn: "After we had been there two or three weeks, we learned where the pubs were that welcomed American fliers. Actually, I never went into a pub where we weren't treated well, once the regulars noted we weren't troublemakers. Many of them told us they counted our ships leaving on missions, and on return again. They were very concerned about our well-being. I also enjoyed the dances at a large hall in Cambridge. The girls were good dancers and the band played music that was popular in the States. They served beer at the dances, and there was a brand called Nut Brown Ale that was pretty heady stuff, so one had to be careful about how much one drank. We had to be back to catch the shuttle truck by eleven P.M., as many of the flight crews were on the alert list for the morning mission."

Ira Eakin also learned to be very careful with the local waters: "They had a beer, Worthington Ale. I drank that and I drank a lot of scotch and soda. I got drunk one time on Irish potato whiskey and I'll never do that again. Me and this buddy of mine, ol' Owen M. Close, we went out to the pub and they'd run out of their ration, so we had a few big mugs of that mild-and-bitter—the stuff they should pour back in the horse—and we got to drinking that and chasing it with Irish whiskey. I thought I was gonna die for a whole week later. Ol' Close slept in the bunk across from me, and he had a little bald spot on top of his head, and first thing every morning he'd put on his little GI cap to cover that bald spot and keep his head from getting cold. Hell, for two weeks later, he'd raise up in bed and he'd put that cap on and he'd grab his head and he'd say, 'Oh, shit.' You could tell he was suffering. That was the last time we ever tried that Irish whiskey."

A Lancaster flight engineer named Leonard Thompson flew his tour with 550 Squadron, based at Waltham in Lincolnshire. "On stand-downs, if we didn't want to go as far as Grimsby or Scunthorpe, we went to the village pub near the airfield. The beer was lousy, but we had a marvelous choir there. The ground crew knew all the old Air Force songs. I think the dirty ones shocked the regulars, but they treated us wonderfully well."

. . . tonight our orders are, 'Bomb the centre of Bremen; make it uninhabitable for the workers.' England! Cricket! Huh! Justifiable? I do not know. I only know that I shall kill women and children soon.

–from *Journeys into Night*, by Don Charlwood

I am a man/ More sinned against than sinning.

–from *King Lear*, Act III, Sc. 2, by William Shakespeare

right: The David Alston
family of Lodge Farm,
Lavenham in WWII,
hosts to the 487BG,
below: *Royal Flush*, a
100BG B-17 down
near Clamart, France,
August 11, 1944.

Every American who served in wartime Britain experienced an air raid or knew someone who did. Ira Eakin told of a GI who was on leave in London when the bombs began to fall: "He was with a girl in this big park, and he threw his body over her and saved her life, and they gave him the Silver Star. Only he didn't put his body over her to save her life. He was doing something else. Boy, we laughed about that."

An Air Force major, similarly placed, was more punctilious: "He was shacking up with a girl in an apartment in London when there was an air-raid warning. He got out of the sack, walked over to the mantel, and put his dog tags on. He didn't care who he was caught in bed with, so long as somebody knew who the hell he was."

Alan Forman had only sixty miles to travel from his base at Elsham Wolds when he went on leave to his hometown near the Wash. "My father was a First World War soldier in the Lincolnshire Regiment. The older chaps like him had to do something, like fire-watching or Air Raid Precautions, and he was a fire-watcher. The sirens went one night and he made me get dressed and go downstairs. We went out and I was looking up and saw a Heinkel 111 in the moonlight. I said, 'He's just dropped some bombs,' but my father laughed it off. Then there was a rushing noise, which suddenly stopped, and all around 'Pop, pop, pop.' They were incendiaries, and one dropped about five yards away. We were lying in the gutter by this time. Everything went quiet for a while, and then fires started up in the roofs of houses and shops. It did a lot of damage in that little town. I thought, 'Well, bugger this,' and went back off leave. They never saw another enemy aircraft. That was it: that was their war."

The V-1 flying bombs, or doodlebugs as the British called them, brought a new dimension to the air-raid stories. "The Germans used to send those damned buzz bombs over," said navigator Frank Nelson of the 487th Bomb Group. "They sounded like a BT-13, and as long as you heard them, no sweat. But when that sound cut out, you knew it was coming down. This one came at night and it sounded like it cut out right over our field. We had slit trenches outside of the Nissen huts there, and you saw nothing but bare feet and white assholes heading for those trenches."

Throughout his time with the "Rackheath Aggies," pilot Keith Newhouse kept a diary of his leisure hours that provides as good a guide to a young American's impressions of the English wartime scene as any journalist could write; its contents might, with minor variations, have equally applied to the experiences of men from Canada, Australia, South Africa, and other far-flung lands of the old British Empire and Commonwealth who flew and fought from England in those days.

"Thursday, April 13, 1944," Newhouse noted. "We had time off today and wandered into Norwich early, got off the bus in the middle of town and just ambled about. The streets are narrow, the sidewalks narrower and the shops flush with the walk. Traffic, of course, flows opposite to ours, and bikes are more of a hazard than cars. Little side streets meander off in every direction, but still and all orientation is easy because everything branches from the center of town. The points of interest are all extremely old buildings and churches. Shopping is done by sweating out long lines outside the shops, which have little to sell. What they do have is valued in coupons. Not 'How much does it cost?' but 'How many coupons?'

"In the towns one can't help noticing the number of baby carriages that crowd the walks. Women with perambulators and two or three little mites swarm through the streets. These Englishmen may be away to the wars most of the time, but they surely aren't wasting any leave time or shooting many blanks.

"The tea-shop was a flight of stairs down from street level, very cramped and informal. The brew was excellent, and we had a sort of gingerbread with raisins, and toast with honey. The honey was tangy, milky in color and granulated. I prefer it to our own. The assortment of crumpets, cookies and the like were rather poor and I imagine rationing has done that, but we shall undoubtedly return.

"Lou went in search of some books for his little son. He picked up A. A. Milne's *When We Were Very Young* and *Now We Are Six*. The two of us laughed and chuckled all the way home swapping the stories back and forth."

"Sunday, April 16. Trees are popping buds, flowers are in bloom and fruit trees are

Mrs Kirby's weekly food ration comprised four ounces of bacon; two ounces of butter plus four ounces of margarine or lard; two ounces of tea; eight ounces of sugar; one shilling and tuppence worth of meat, which amounted to about thirteen ounces or less, depending on price; and a cheese ration which varied considerably during the war, but averaged around two or three ounces a week. In addition she was entitled to one egg; one packet of dried eggs; eight ounces of jam; and twelve ounces of chocolate or sweets. Milk was 'controlled' at around two or two and a half pints per person per week. Potatoes, bread and fresh vegetables were not rationed, but the latter were scarce and distributed on a controlled basis. Tinned and packet foods were on 'points'. Mrs Kirby was entitled to twenty points per four week period. One packet of breakfast cereal, one tin

all a-blossom. It is lovely and growing more so. The thing that forces itself on the observer here is the system of fences. They appear in all forms, sizes and lengths. Every little plot has its perimeter defined by some manner of pickets, lathes, wire, stone wall or shrubbery—anything to form a dividing line. A Westerner would feel he had been set down in somebody's idea of what a child's world should be like. The whole scene gives a rather cozy feeling."

"Saturday, May 13. The London leave was perfect. The number of cabs and the crowds on the street impressed us at first. I've never seen as many cabs, even in Chicago. We never had any trouble getting one, and they were cheap until blackout time. Then the sky was the limit. A trip that cost about thirty cents in daylight ran about $1 after dark. We didn't have much trouble getting a hotel room and had excellent food in one of the officers' clubs. We bought some clothes down at the big PX and then went in search of liquor. We finally bought Booth's dry gin and some good scotch at $13 a fifth for the gin and $17 for the whiskey. So, for about $50 we managed to get stinking enough not to be interested in the stuff next day, and to go to *Something For The Boys* the following evening. It was a fair show, but the chorus saved the day. What seductive legs, and of course we were only three rows from the front.

"We traveled to Lou's field by train.

Their cars are called coaches, and are about half the length of ours. Six people sit in a nice first class compartment. The seats are feather soft, with arm-rests, and the upholstery is a delicate, flowery broadcloth sort of weave. The toilets are twice the size of American train closets and kept spick-and-span. Most of our travel back to home was in the top of a double-decker bus. We had box seats for the lovely panorama that is the English countryside. This island is beautiful."

"I've heard a lot of bad remarks," said Ira Eakin, "about the English people, but don't believe it. They're great in my book. They really treated us great. They would come around those bases every weekend and invite so many GIs to their homes, and a lot of times they'd take you out there and fix you a good meal, and they were doing without themselves, we found out later." Paul Sink agreed:"The English made a lot of sacrifices for the Americans there in World War Two."

Most men in their twenties are mentally resilient: they adapt readily to change. Even so, the bomber crews couldn't fail to notice the extraordinary contrast between their operational environment and their free time on the ground. "The unusual thing was," Jack Clift remarked, "you'd be on ops one night and at a party next night. You'd think, It's unreal, this. There we were, up dicing with death last night and here we are at The Horse and Jockey, living it up. It was very strange."

of pilchards, half a pound of chocolate biscuits, one pound of rice, and one tin of grade three salmon, added up to twenty 'points', and so would exhaust Mrs Kirby's entitlement for a whole month. At twenty-four points for a one pound tin, stewed steak was a luxury available only to housewives with several ration books at their disposal. For a nation of tea drinkers, the meagre ration of two ounces a week was probably the greatest hardship. Otherwise, the draconian rationing system equalized hunger, as it were; no one starved, and the health of the British people actually improved, which said much about the pre-war British diet, inequalities and deprivations of the unemployed and the poorly paid.

—from *Yesterday's Gone*, by N. J. Crisp

far left above: Former 207 Sqn. mid-upper gunner, Jim Barfoot, left above: Former 57 Sqn. wireless operator/ air gunner, Roland Hammersley, far left below: A disguised pillbox at Leiston in 1944, left below: Percy Kindred, of the 390BG Museum.

To describe warplanes in terms of their statistics—weight, length and wingspan, bombloads and armament, power plants and cruising speeds—is for books of reference. The figures are factual and give no cause for argument. To offer an opinion on less definable characteristics—maneuverability, effectiveness, feel, or appearance—is to be subjective and to risk making hackles rise somewhere in the world; to compare like with like—the B-17, say, with the B-24, the Lancaster with the Halifax, the Spitfire with the Hurricane, or the P-47 with the P-51—and to state that either airplane was superior, is to court an argument with the other's champions. Veterans of the air war have it in common that they had, and had to have, faith in their aircraft; that was the plane that saw them through their missions: they will regard it with affection and guard its reputation evermore. The opinions, therefore, that follow in this chapter should be read with that loyalty in mind.

There was a time after graduation when Ray Wild's ambition was to fly a pursuit plane. "But a little major got up and asked if any of us red-blooded Americans wanted to get into action right now. We raised our hands, and they sent us to Sebring, Florida, on B-17s. We knew nothing about them. They looked like great big lumbering things, and we weren't too happy, really. They used to send you to gunnery range, for the waist and tail gunners to shoot at targets, and you realized it was steady—a great platform to shoot from. We started to like the airplane. That thing

THE HARDWARE

"War stories leave me cold. That author never took off in a fully loaded B-24. Telling of the grace with which they fly when the gear comes up! About that time, the pilot is sweating out flying speed, and when the flaps are milked off, the damned thing sort of wants to settle in again. We're loaded far above the designed capacity and she just won't fly good until the bombs are away or lots of gas is burned."

Keith Newhouse, pilot, 467BG

"I guess the B-24 was a reasonably good airplane, but they had a bomb bay fuel tank in them and an electric landing gear right close to that tank and I've seen those things blow up on takeoff. You'd get a leak in that tank, see, and when you flipped your gear switch, an arc from the electric motor would set it off."

Ira Eakin, crew chief, 91BG

could be ten feet off the ground and hold steady. You put it on automatic pilot and it held steady. You didn't do it, of course, but you could.

"Now, the B-24 was ten miles faster, it cruised at one-seventy, but it had a Davis wing, which was a great wing, except that if you got a hit in one wing that doubled the stress on the other. It could get hit lightly and go down. A B-17 you could chop in little pieces and that sonofabitch would come back. It would fly when it shouldn't fly. We lost eight feet of a wing one time and twelve feet off the stabilizer, and it handled the same way. A little sluggish, maybe, but it was fine. You could lose two engines on one side in a 17 and so long as you turned into the live engines you could fly it. Everybody knew that the plane would get back. If they could stay in it and stay alive, they knew they'd get back. The only way you wouldn't was with a direct hit or with a wing blown off. You got a great affinity with it. Of course, the B-24 pilots said the same thing. For them the 24 was the best airplane in the world."

For an aircraft designed in 1934 as the very first all-metal four-engined monoplane bomber, the "Fort" had a marvelous career. Don Maffett realized its robust qualities on the first of his forty missions with the 452nd Bomb Group. "The left wheel was shot off, but I didn't know that, and I landed on one wheel. The airplane had three hundred and fifty flak holes in it. The B-17 could take a lot of punishment—I think far more than the B-24. Shot up or in good shape, the B-17 was pretty consistent. You'd come in over

the fence at a hundred and ten, and it would stall out at ninety-two or ninety-three. It gave you a tremendous feeling of confidence."

There used to be a tale that when a prototype bomber was wheeled out of the factory, you would see a group of men with slide rules walking anxiously around it. The answer to the question as to who those men might be, and what they were about, was that they were the designers, trying to find a place to put the crew. Don Maffett, for one, had some reservations about the pilot's accommodation in the B-17: "It was very cramped. There was very little space between the seats. With the armor plate, your heavy fleece-lined equipment, parachute, and so forth, it was almost impossible to squeeze between the seats and get out if you had to."

Maffett's comments could be applied with equal force to the Avro Lancaster: a price had to be paid for that slender, streamlined shape. There was little room in the cabin and the fuselage, and moving fore or aft was like competing in an obstacle race. It was for this reason, throughout his tour with 550 Squadron, that flight engineer Leonard Thompson never used his seat. "It was a bench," he said, "that folded down from the side of the aircraft, and you pulled a short tube out for a footrest. If there was ever an emergency, they would be a problem, and the time it took to get them out of the way might make the difference between escaping with your life and not."

Group Captain (later Lord) Leonard Cheshire, VC, flew a hundred missions in

pages 134-35: New B-17Gs at an air depot in England awaiting field modification and their turn in the air war, far left: DeHavilland Mosquito assembly, left: B-17 maintenance at Eye, the 490BG base, below left: A Halifax being repaired after incurring battle damage in raids of November 1942, below: recognition views of the Armstrong Whitworth Whitley bomber.

Necessity makes even the timid brave.

—Sallust

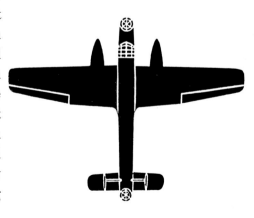

137

The Lancaster bomber was the best of its class which appeared in the Second World War. It had the capacity to lift a ten-ton bomb. It was robust and reliable in action and, on targets of equal risk, suffered a lower casualty rate than its equivalent versions, the Halifax and the Stirling. Like them, it had not, however, the capacity to survive in combat with opposing fighters.

—from *The Bombing Offensive Against Germany*, by Noble Frankland

God! they're heavy machines, especially on aileron control, you fairly have to heave on them to do just a rate one turn. . . . They're not so very hard to land, but have a bad fault in the tail-wheel shimmer. It seems as though the whole machine is going to shake to pieces. On take-off it has a tendency to swing to port—not very badly though. . . . The approach is as fast as a Spitfire . . . come in at 111 mph. Drag it off the deck on take-off at 100 mph.

—from *Journeys into Night*, by Don Charlwood

Whitleys, Halifaxes, Lancasters, Mosquitoes, and, on occasion, in a Mustang borrowed from one of Brigadier Hunter's Eighth Air Force fighter groups. He was arguably the RAF's most successful bomber pilot. In 1991, he gave a view about the two main British bombers. "One has to be careful when comparing one aircraft with another. I know that those who flew the Halifax and nothing else will stand up and say it was the best aircraft in the wartime RAF, and I completely respect that. But I did two tours on Halifaxes before I flew the Lancaster and the difference was very obvious. The Lanc was a forgiving aircraft. You could make mistakes—I made mistakes—and get away with it. It was a beautiful machine." Most pilots-who, like Cheshire, flew both airplanes would agree with that opinion.

The Halifax was stable, reliable, and solid as a rock, but the early models were not a great success. The Mark I, for example, had trouble with the rudders, which could lock in the airflow and perpetuate a turn. The Lancaster flew faster, higher, farther, and carried greater loads; the majority of pilots found it easier to fly. By early 1943, the Halifaxes were suffering such losses that they were restricted to the shorter or less hazardous operations. They resumed a full share of the main offensive with the arrival of the Mark III, which had redesigned rudders, air-cooled Bristol engines, no front turret, a lower profile dorsal turret, and a much improved performance. "The Mark III was a marvelous aircraft," enthused rear gunner Eric Barnard, half of whose thirty-two mis-

sions with 10 Squadron were in daylight. "It climbed like a rocket and was very maneuverable. I was frightened to death all the time on ops, but I loved the Halifax."

Fred Allen, another rear gunner, agreed with Eric Barnard. "The Lanc got the glory, like the Spitfire and the Fortress, but the Halifax played its part, same as the Hurricane and the Liberator. I was trained on Wellingtons, with the Fraser-Nash gun turret, hydraulically operated, the same as on the Lancaster. The Halifax had the Boulton-Paul turrets, electrically operated. That's typical—train you on one and then put you in another. Just to keep you awake, I suppose. You controlled the Lanc turret with two handles, but the Halifax turret had a joystick, just like in a fighter, with the firing button on top. There were two doors into the turret, and the bulkhead door behind that. You had to get through those to reach where your parachute was stowed."

Like many air war veterans, on both sides of the Atlantic, Allen now suffers when the temperature is low. "It was summertime, and when we went out to the aircraft the sun was still high. You daren't move about much, or you'd start sweating. Then you went up to 20,000 feet and it was twenty degrees below. I'd got more skins on than an onion: long johns, shirt, pullovers, three pairs of socks. There wasn't any heating. The electric suit was all right, if it worked, but my hands were always frozen, and to this day they go white when it's cold. There was a sliding plexiglass panel between the guns, and one on each side of the turret. We used

"You think your plane's badly damaged? You should take a look at ours."

Most allied aircraft in WWII were built mainly by women. left: Factory assembly of DeHavilland Mosquitos, below left: Finishing work on Boeing B-17Gs, below: Riveting wing panels for the Avro Lancaster bomber.

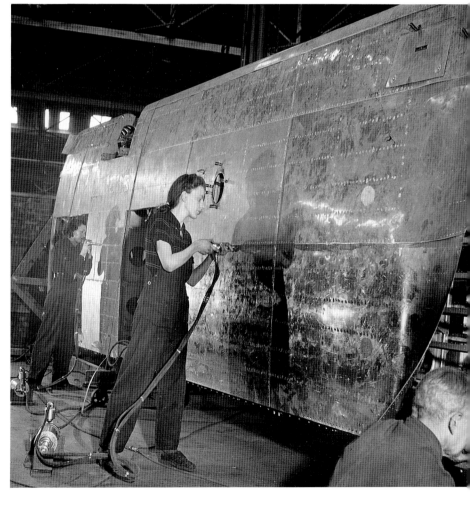

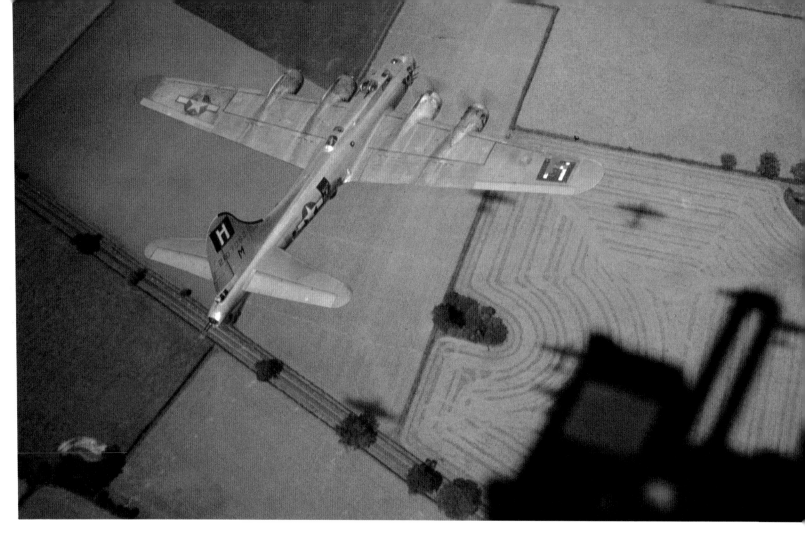

. . . it took a natural athlete, if a small one, to gyrate those Sperry K-2 power turrets around, traversing through range and deflection at the same time, by means of feather-delicate touches on the hand grips of the guns, to get a bead on a German fighter coming from underneath at a skidding angle.

—from *The War Lover*, by John Hersey

to take them out for better visibility, because the least little speck, after you've been looking out for hours in the dark, you were convinced it was a German fighter."

Another ailment to which old RAF bomber men are prone is a degree of deafness known as "Lancaster ear." "The noise level in the Lanc was terrible," said Reg Payne. "We always tried to leave the intercom free for the pilot and gunners, and if I had something to say to the navigator, I had to lift up his helmet and shout it with my mouth against his ear."

"All the Lancasters were needed for operations," said flight engineer Jack Clift, "so at the heavy conversion unit we familiarized ourselves with the procedures in old Stirlings. They were very difficult, a 1930s aeroplane. I didn't like the electrics, they weren't as positive as hydraulics, and the undercarriage was so tall that the pilot couldn't judge his distance off the ground very easily. On one landing we overshot the runway, and went into a ploughed field. We wrote the undercarriage off and got into a lot of trouble from the CO. He said, 'This is terrible,' as though we'd done it on purpose. But the Lancaster was marvelous. We really enjoyed flying the Lancaster. And the Merlins were excellent engines. Beautiful. Over a very long haul—nine, ten, eleven hours—no trouble at all, provided they weren't hit."

Crew chief Ira Eakin witnessed many belly landings by the bombers while he was at Bassingbourn. "I seen a lot of where there were dead personnel in the aircraft, but they'd been killed from flak or enemy fight-

141

above left: A 388BG B-17 returning to Knettishall, below left: A Short Stirling visiting the 94BG base at Rougham, above: A 453BG B-24 over France, below: A bomb dump at the 490BG base at Eye.

In 1942 the government advertised in various American newspapers that it was looking for women to contribute their hair to the war effort. Mary Babnik Brown saw the ad in her local Colorado paper and responded with an inquiry. She quickly recieved a telegram asking for a sample, which she sent. In a few days she received a telegram pleading for her hair. Her long golden tresses were exactly what the officials at the Institute of Technology in Washington needed. Mary's hair was to be used experimentally as cross hairs in a bomb-aiming device known as the Norden bombsight. Her fine, blond, 34-inch hair, which had never been bleached, was unique

ers—they were dead before the crash. There was one crash there where this night crew was to service a B-17 but they only serviced half of it. The story was the guy was drunk when he did it and he never did service the other half. But that was part of the flight crew's check before takeoff—check the fuel load and everything. I never understand why they didn't do that, but apparently they didn't. They started a takeoff with this 17 and they got off the ground with it, loaded up with five-hundred-pound delayed-action bombs, and this heavy wing started coming down and dragging on the runway, and it cartwheeled that thing right into a bunch of tents where these people that worked nights were sleeping. Of course it broke up and ex-ploded. Every time they tried to go in and get those guys out the bombs were going off. The only guy that come out of it was the copilot. They say he was burning from his

feet to the top of his head when he come out. I think he lived."

Of the B-17, Eakin said this: "It was the greatest. I know we gotta have progress and all that, but I don't think they'll ever build one as great as that was for its time. I've seen those things just absolutely riddled. I saw one where a Me 109 went right through the fuselage at the waist windows. There was just a strip of metal on top of the fuselage and a strip on the bottom holding the tail on that thing. The tail was setting up there and wig-gling around, and all the control cables go right up the top of the fuselage and this Me 109 went under 'em and didn't cut any of 'em. They flew deep out of France with that

thing and way back into England, and when the pilot hit the runway with it, he held the tail up, and when he let it down the fuselage broke in half. Of course, he had casualties. Wiped out both the waist gunners and I think he got the top gunner too. But it's unbelievable the punishment that airplane could take and keep flying. Several occasions, those Me 109s would run out of ammo trying to shoot a 17 down and they'd fly along beside him and look at him in amazement at how that thing was staying up there."

"There was always a controversy about the B-17 and the B-24," said Paul Sink. "I flew in them both and I always thought the B-17 was the better airplane. It was a very good aircraft. But the B-24 was a good airplane too." So it was: with its great endurance and bomb bay capacity, it was effective in the Pacific theater, and as a U-boat destroyer it was the RAF Coastal Command's most successful aircraft.

Frank Nelson was another flier who had operational experience of both aircraft. In July 1944, he was midway through his tour as a navigator on B-24s when his group—the 487th at Lavenham in Suffolk—reequipped with B-17s. Nelson was glad of that, because "in the B-17s we could get up to over twenty thousand, and this made quite a difference as far as flak was concerned. Also it ran our

and perfect for the task at hand. The Norden became the mechanical computing high-altitude bombsight used in the B-17, B-24, B-29, and other U.S. bomber aircraft of WWII.

left: A factory-fresh Martin B-26 Marauder, a type used in quantity by 9AF medium bomb groups based in the south of East Anglia.

THE NORDEN BOMBSIGHT

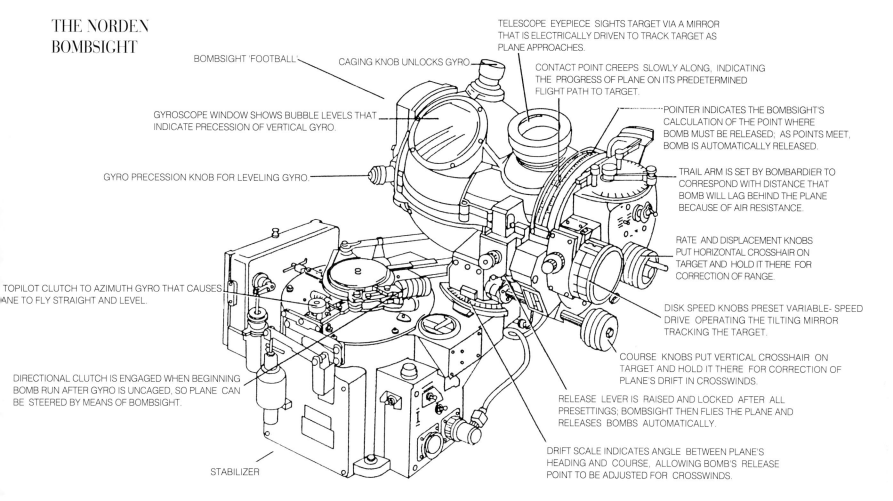

TELESCOPE EYEPIECE SIGHTS TARGET VIA A MIRROR THAT IS ELECTRICALLY DRIVEN TO TRACK TARGET AS PLANE APPROACHES.

BOMBSIGHT 'FOOTBALL'

CAGING KNOB UNLOCKS GYRO

CONTACT POINT CREEPS SLOWLY ALONG, INDICATING THE PROGRESS OF PLANE ON ITS PREDETERMINED FLIGHT PATH TO TARGET.

GYROSCOPE WINDOW SHOWS BUBBLE LEVELS THAT INDICATE PRECESSION OF VERTICAL GYRO.

POINTER INDICATES THE BOMBSIGHT'S CALCULATION OF THE POINT WHERE BOMB MUST BE RELEASED; AS POINTS MEET, BOMB IS AUTOMATICALLY RELEASED.

GYRO PRECESSION KNOB FOR LEVELING GYRO.

TRAIL ARM IS SET BY BOMBARDIER TO CORRESPOND WITH DISTANCE THAT BOMB WILL LAG BEHIND THE PLANE BECAUSE OF AIR RESISTANCE.

RATE AND DISPLACEMENT KNOBS PUT HORIZONTAL CROSSHAIR ON TARGET AND HOLD IT THERE FOR CORRECTION OF RANGE.

TOPILOT CLUTCH TO AZIMUTH GYRO THAT CAUSES ANE TO FLY STRAIGHT AND LEVEL.

DISK SPEED KNOBS PRESET VARIABLE- SPEED DRIVE OPERATING THE TILTING MIRROR TRACKING THE TARGET.

COURSE KNOBS PUT VERTICAL CROSSHAIR ON TARGET AND HOLD IT THERE FOR CORRECTION OF PLANE'S DRIFT IN CROSSWINDS.

DIRECTIONAL CLUTCH IS ENGAGED WHEN BEGINNING BOMB RUN AFTER GYRO IS UNCAGED, SO PLANE CAN BE STEERED BY MEANS OF BOMBSIGHT.

RELEASE LEVER IS RAISED AND LOCKED AFTER ALL PRESETTINGS; BOMBSIGHT THEN FLIES THE PLANE AND RELEASES BOMBS AUTOMATICALLY.

DRIFT SCALE INDICATES ANGLE BETWEEN PLANE'S HEADING AND COURSE, ALLOWING BOMB'S RELEASE POINT TO BE ADJUSTED FOR CROSSWINDS.

STABILIZER

true airspeed up to two hundred knots or a little better, which meant we were out of the flak that much quicker."

W. W. Ford agreed with Nelson's view. "The 24s couldn't hold the altitude the 17s could hold," he said. "The flak was heavier down at their altitude and the fighters would pick on them before us, because usually the P-51s were above us in more strength than they were around the 24s. They got clobbered a lot worse than we did." Ford, however, does remember one elderly B-17 at Podington of which it was rumored that if anybody pulled a certain cotter key in the bomb bay the whole airplane would immediately disintegrate. "I could believe it," said Ford. "That B-17 always sounded like it was gonna fall apart."

In the same way that the early Halifaxes had to bomb below the Lancasters, the B-24s usually operated several thousand feet below the B-17s. At 20,000 feet, the B-24 became too unstable to fly in close formation, and its slow rate of ascent gave rise to other problems, as Keith Newhouse found when he took off from Rackheath in *Wallowing Wilbur* in late April 1944, and began a long climb through the overcast. At 12,000 feet, ice was building up on all the frontal surfaces and, a few moments later, *Wallowing Wilbur* stalled. Newhouse regained control, the copilot opened the throttles and lowered a little flap to give the airfoils more lift, but the ice continued to accrete. The port wing went down, and the aircraft lost two thousand feet of altitude. Twice more, Newhouse tried to climb above the icing

below: The cockpit panel of an Avro Lancaster, this one equipped with a dual control conversion kit, left, top to bottom: Lancaster *City of Lincoln*, maintained and still flown by the RAF Battle of Britain Memorial Flight at RAF Coningsby, the positions of the bomb aimer, wireless operator and rear gunner.

144

The aircraft is designed
for manoeuvres
appropriate to a heavy
bomber and care must
be taken to avoid
imposing excessive loads
in recovering from dives
and in turns at high
speed. Spinning and
aerobatics are not
permitted.

Pilot's Notes, Avro
Lancaster

An aircraft designed by
engineers and built by
craftsmen and women
for heroes to fly.

—Sir George Edwards on
the Lancaster

level, and each time was frustrated. By then, the airplane had taken on so much ice that he could not maintain height, let alone increase it. He turned back to Rackheath and, shortly afterward, the force was instructed by radio to abandon the mission.

Early in his tour with 44 Squadron at Waddington, Laurence Pilgrim was en route to Duisburg in the Ruhr, when an airplane below him exploded and turned his Lancaster upside down. Aerobatics in a fully laden bomber were to be avoided, especially in the dark and with the gyro instruments toppled, but Pilgrim had no choice: he had either to roll out with ailerons and rudders, or pull the

above: A Lancaster II, fitted with the Bristol Hercules engines for greater power than that provided by the Merlin-powered Lancs. below: An Avro Lancaster Mk I back from the daylight raid on Augsburg of April 17, 1942. The raid was an experiment by Arthur Harris and a costly failure for RAF Bomber Command.

stick back as in the last half of a loop. Ordering his flight engineer to reduce the power, Pilgrim chose the half-loop as the less unpleasant prospect. The engineer, as it happened, was lying on the cabin roof; falling into place, he knocked the throttles back—exactly at the moment when Pilgrim, recovering, wanted them wide open. Having got their act together, the crew flew on to Duisburg. Since that occurrence, Pilgrim has maintained that the Lancaster was fully aerobatic.

A few months later, a 12 Squadron pilot had an experience that was, if anything, even more alarming. On the last of the Hamburg firestorm raids in *Operation Gomorrah*, the approach to the target was barred by towering thunderclouds, one of which he entered while avoiding flak. Instantly, the Lancaster was covered in a heavy layer of ice; the controls were immobilized, the aircraft stalled, flipped onto its back, and went into a spin. While the crew were tossed about the cabin like ice cubes in a shaker, the pilot fought to gain control. Ten thousand feet down, he felt a sudden snap, which worried him, although the elevators answered to his hands. Trying to steer the airplane, he realized what had happened: the ailerons had been torn off in the spin. So, it transpired, had the aerials, pieces of the turrets, and the flaps. Steering with the rudders and bursts of outboard engine, he flew the aircraft back to Lincolnshire, evading searchlights and a fighter on the way, and made a flapless landing. It was, as Leonard Cheshire said, a most forgiving aircraft.

above: A Lancaster factory line showing the production facility on September 7, 1943.

147

MUD AND MUSCLE

"The squadron was based at Ludford Magna, northeast of Lincoln. It was a pretty soggy spot. We called it Mudford Stagna."

Pete Johnson, pilot, 101 Sqn.

below: Lancaster crew slog through a muddy lane on the way from their crew room to the van that will take them to their aircraft.

THE FALL OF 1942 was not the best of seasons for turning farmland into bomber bases, and the remark of an airfield engineer came right from the heart: "Where there's construction, there's mud; and where there's war there's mud; where there's construction *and* war, there's just plain hell."

Each airfield needed 100,000 tons of aggregate, many miles of drainage pipes, and concrete foundations for some four hundred buildings. John Skilleter, the evacuee from London, watched the construction of the Eighth Air Force bases in the quiet Suffolk countryside. At every opportunity he accompanied the driver of a Bedford truck on his haulage trips. "We collected shingle and carted it at breakneck speed to the airfield sites. The drivers did the maximum number of trips per day because they were paid ac-

cordingly. Every truck owner in the area was earning good money at that time. As the Americans got into their stride, so the airfields multiplied: Eye, Great Ashfield, Leiston, Framlingham, Mendlesham, Boxted, Debach, and many others. The U.S. Army engineers were quick-fire, happy-go-lucky guys who never failed to hand out chewing gum to us sweet-starved kids.

"When the B-17s arrived," Skilleter continued, "I would sit on top of the truck and watch the splendor of the squadrons moving in line astern around the perimeter track, with baseball-capped gunners in the waist positions and concerned-looking pilots fingering their throat-mikes as they talked to the tower. Ground crews squatted on the tarmac by the runway and waved them off with V-signs. Sometimes, about an hour after takeoff, the aborts would trickle in—aircraft

with feathered props. Jeeps tore alongside the machines as they turned into the hardstandings. At other times, the only activity would be around a grounded B-17, as mechanics tried to cuss its entrails into life."

All wartime fliers, of whatever nationality, held a high opinion of the men and women who maintained their aircraft. In 1943, Air Chief Marshal Harris sent a message to his ground crews: "On January 20th, 1,030 aircraft were serviceable out of an establishment of 1,038. When the work has to be done under such trying conditions this record is almost incredible. My thanks and congratulations to all concerned in this achievement. You, after the aircrew, are playing the leading part in getting on with this war."

It was not for the ground crews to face the fighters or the flak (although many would have liked to have the chance); they expected no glory and, in that, their expectations were fulfilled. For the RAF men—the fitters and riggers, instrument "bashers" and electricians, radar mechanics and armorers—who kept the bombers flying, and for the WAAF radar plotters, radio operators, parachute packers, and motor transport drivers, there would be no medal to show the part they played in World War II, although, as Harris later wrote: "Every clerk, butcher or baker in the rear of the armies overseas had a campaign medal." They and their colleagues in the USAAF worked long hours in harsh conditions, and all they asked was that "their" plane and its crew came back to base. That was enough reward—that, the good

opinion of the sergeant, and an occasional "thank you" from the flying men. Certainly, without them there would have been no glory, nor any victory.

"We never had a single component failure in the aircraft during our tour," said Tony Partridge, a Halifax bomb-aimer. "The ground crew were marvelous; there was one little mechanic who used to run along and kiss each engine, just before we started up. Funny, because he wasn't flying, but he used to do it every time."

Laurence Pilgrim remembered that his Lancaster ground crew entertained a seemingly misogynous superstition: "They just wouldn't let a WAAF come onto the hardstanding on the night of an operation. If a WAAF driver came out with a message for the pilot—last-minute instructions from control or something—one of them would take the note from her and deliver it himself. They believed that we wouldn't come back if a WAAF set foot on our hardstanding."

"It never bothered me," said Ira Eakin, "to get out there and really put out to get a plane going. I'd work as high as thirty-six hours without sleep, and just lay down on a warm engine and go to sleep, you got so tired. But I never thought nothing about it. Fact is, I believed in what I was doing. And we always had good base commanders. I was lucky that way, I guess."

Colonel Dale O. Smith was one of those commanders. When he was assigned to the 384th Bomb Group at Grafton Underwood in November 1943, he soon understood why the base was known as Grafton Undermud.

The rain slanted under the wing on a raw northeast wind. Of Cambridgeshire we had only an impression screened through the deluge—somber flatness, and mud; mud oozing up over the edge of the asphalt circle where we were parked; mud in the tread of the jeep, which rolled away on twin tracks of ocher, leaving us marooned; a vast plain, or lake, of mud stretching off toward a cluster of barely visible buildings.

—from *The War Lover*, by John Hersey

below: Nissen huts seem to be sinking into the mud at Old Buckenham.

149

The stars were out that night. I liked that very much because it meant a hard freeze and out of the mud for at least two or three days. Also it sent a message to the combat crews: get ready for a mission in the morning. With that in mind I set out my mission clothes and equipment. Most combat men developed superstitions about clothes or some special talisman they always carried on a raid. I remember one gunner who wore the same coveralls each trip and refused to have them washed. Somehow the unwashed coveralls had become his security blanket.

—from *Combat Crew*, by John Comer

If there comes a little thaw,/ Still the air is chill and raw,/ Here and there a patch of snow, Dirtier than the ground below,/ Dribbles down a marshy flood; Ankle-deep you stick in mud/ In the meadows while you sing, "This is Spring."

—"A Spring Growl," by C. P. Cranch

"We had bicycles to get around the base, but the mud was so bad we mostly had to carry them."

Sam Young, bombardier, 452BG

"The clay soil held the rain," he wrote, "and the place was a sea of sticky, brown muck. Everyone slogged to the mess halls in overshoes and parked them at the doors, but mud invaded every building and dried on the floors. Tires of the trucks tracked mud onto the taxiways and hardstands where the B-17s were parked, and mud accumulated on their wheels. There were instances of landing gear sticking in the up position when the mud froze. Something had to be done."

Smith did something. Digging in the mire on one of the base roads, he came to solid concrete, and set every man to work with spades and shovels. "There were miles of roads, but we had thousands of people. They grumbled, but they shoveled, and the roads began to clear. I put out an order that trucks were to stay on the pavement and pass only at the concrete turnouts."

After one sergeant truckdriver had been busted to private on the spot, there were no more offenders. Morale seemed to improve, men could ride on bicycles and walk without overshoes. Then Smith discovered that a fleet of mud-caked dump trucks were engaged in moving massive piles of earth from one site to another on the base, and undoing all the efforts of the last two weeks.

"The mud movers," Smith recorded, "were working for the Duke of Buccleuch, who owned our base. I tried the phone but the Duke was shooting in Scotland. I requested his manager to stop the trucks but he said he could do nothing without the Duke's approval. I instructed my ground exec. to put guards on the gates to those mud fields and not let a single truck pass. All hell broke loose. High-ranking Brits from the Air Ministry called me: the Duke was a member of the Royal family. Generals from Eighth Air Force HQ admonished me: the rental agreement allowed the Duke to use our roads, I was injuring relations with our allies, etc."

The colonel stood firm: no more ducal trucks while he was in command. Daily, he expected transfer orders to arrive. None did. The trucks and the power shovel stayed immobile in the fields, and were still there eleven months later when he left Grafton Underwood—no longer under mud.

"That weather!" exclaimed Ira Eakin. "I asked a lot of English people and they said it wasn't like that before the war started. All those explosives going off and all that kinda stuff. But the three years that I was there you could take all the sunshine and bunch it up and you wouldn't have made a month of it. It was unbelievable. We'd take off from Bassingbourn and you could see for miles, and you wouldn't be up there five minutes and you couldn't see nowhere. You'd just keep on climbing till you climbed out of that stuff. You might come back and it would be clear. But it was raining, foggy, snowing—something—most of the time."

Throughout his tour with the 92nd Bomb Group at Podington, Ray Wild called every B-17 he flew *Mizpah* (Hebrew, meaning "May God protect us while we are apart from one another"), although the name was only ever painted on the first. After that orig-

150

inal *Mizpah*, he flew a total of nine different aircraft. "If you got one shot up, maybe they'd repair it or use it for spare parts, and the next day you'd be flying a different airplane. It could have flown ninety-two missions, or this could have been its first, but the ground crews were so great, it didn't make much difference."

Larry Bird has always been grateful to the men who tended the aircraft of the 493rd Bomb Group based at Debach. "Most of those guys," he said, "were off the farm two years before, but we wouldn't be here now if it wasn't for them and the conscientious way they worked. They would start on those airplanes whatever time you came in and work on them continuously until you took off next morning on a mission. They never stopped. I've seen guys work at night with a flashlight in their mouths so they could have both hands free. Cold as hell, raining, foggy. I know I feel really warm about those guys."

One of those guys was armorer Sam Burchell of the 448th Bomb Group at Seething: "In the evening, there'd be a message from the top sergeant when to start loading, and we'd go to our particular planes and put the bombs on—fragmentation, five-hundred-pounders or whatever. That generally took from eleven at night to four or five in the morning. When the planes left, we'd go and have breakfast and then sleep till noon or so. The fifty-caliber guns tended to jam on occasion, which could be from the cold, and there were problems with the hydraulically operated turrets, but nothing spectacular. I wasn't that much of a mechanic, but the guys

who were a little older had been working on gas stations and that, and they could fix those things."

However careful and skillful the armorers might be, there was always the danger of a "hang-up" in the air. In the Lancaster and Halifax, with their capacious bomb bays, this was seldom more than an inconvenience: the offending bomb could usually be shaken off, or released when the aircraft was at a lower, warmer altitude. In the narrow bomb bay of a Fortress, however, where the bombs were stacked one upon another, it could be more embarrassing. Half Larry Bird's load of five-hundred-pounders, on one such occasion, were logjammed by a lower, hung-up bomb. Armed with a screwdriver and a relay of portable oxygen bottles, he set out to resolve the situation. "I bet I was down there twenty-five or thirty minutes," he recalled, "on this little catwalk, just inches wide, with the bomb doors open, trying to get that thing away, and the longer I was down there the madder I got. There wasn't enough room to wear a parachute, and the airplane was really bouncing around. Those bombs were charged, and ready to explode. There was a lot of drag on the airplane with the bomb doors being open, and the pilot was struggling to stay with the formation. He kept sending messages back, like 'Get on with it, Bird, damn it!' I was working like the devil and it was really cold. Finally, I got that shackle to release, and they all went. It just so happened we were passing over the American lines, but I didn't know that at the time."

above: Sweeping mud from your boots was just part of the routine at most USAAF and RAF bases in WWII England.

Talk about flying blind. It took me about ten minutes to do a one-minute walk over to the Admin block, feeling my way along the asphalt path with those heavy sloggers. I'd get off in the mud once in a while—though actually it was less soupy than usual, as we had had five days of good weather—and then feel my way back onto the hardtop; and poking along that way I got there.

—from *The War Lover*, by John Hersey

AIRCREW

"The more I work with the crew the more satisfied I am that I've been extremely lucky. The way they take care of their guns and how anxious they are to learn makes me very happy. Wilhite and Twogood have been able to do something about most every mechanical trouble we've had. Every man can handle any turret. I believe our chances of coming through are good."

Keith Newhouse, pilot, 467BG

When the Lord created man, he gave him two ends, one to sit on, and one to think with. Ever since that day man's success or failure has been dependent on the one he uses the most. It has been always, and is now, a case of heads you win and tails you lose.

–from *Tee Emm*

right: Members of the Joe McCarthy crew of 617 (Dambusters) Squadron photographed at Scampton near Lincoln. It was from this base that 617 Squadron flew the famous raid of May 16, 1943, attacking and breaching the great dams of the Ruhr.

IN WORLD WAR II, the most effective fighting units were usually small—submarine crews, infantry platoons, commandos, and bomber crews. Of these, it could be said that the men who crewed the bombers caused more damage to the enemy and had a greater impact on the outcome of the conflict than any number of the rest. Most of the aircrews were volunteers (in the RAF, they all were), intelligent, fit, and highly trained. Each knew he was essential to the team, whether one of nine or ten in a Fortress or a Liberator, or one of seven in a British bomber; he knew that a mistake by any one could mean the death of all. Their interdependence was a welding influence.

When a man was trained in the USAAF to become a pilot, a navigator, or a bombardier, his training as an officer proceeded hand in hand with his training as a flier: if he flunked in either aspect he didn't graduate. It followed that those members of the crew, including the copilot, in an Eighth Air Force bomber were commissioned officers, while the gunners were enlisted men with the rank of sergeant. In the RAF, it was different, and many crews were entirely composed of NCOs, while some were of mixed ranks, with the pilot, of whatever rank, always being the captain of the aircraft.

"It was really a matter of luck," said Laurence Pilgrim of the RAF, "whether you got a good crew or not to start with. Once they were formed, it was up to the captain to mold them into the sort of crew he wanted. In my opinion, if the crew didn't turn out well, it was the captain's fault. It was essen-

"I spent this evening with Sully. He is going to his tail gunner's funeral tomorrow, after which I hope to see him for a few evening beers."

Keith Newhouse, pilot, 467BG

tial to go out together quite often, to have a drink together and be as friendly as possible. Of course, the pilot had to have the crew's respect—not as NCOs to officer, but as crew to captain—so that if he said something in the air, they did it without question."

Dave Shelhamer of the 303rd Bomb Group also saw a need for a modicum of discipline: "I made a statement that if anybody on this crew fouls up, and it was some little thing, admonition and that would be it. But anything serious, and that person would be off the crew. Now, whether they believed I would do that I don't know. But when Keaton really pulled a lulu and I summarily removed him from the crew, it was a kind of shock to them. After that I had a crew that worked like a well-oiled machine. They were just beautiful."

A typical RAF all-NCO crew was that of Alan Forman, who flew thirteen operations with 103 Squadron in the final stages of the war. Forman was the son of a Lincolnshire farmhand, and he had never expected to be a bomber captain. "I put in for air gunner, but there was an old first war flier, an air commodore, on the selection board, and he told me I ought to try for pilot. I told him I left school at fourteen and my maths was pretty poor, but he said not to worry about that. I was very lucky. I passed the course in Canada, while a lot of people failed. They ended up as navigators or bomb-aimers. I went through operational training and got my own crew: a Scotsman, two Yorkshiremen, three Australians, and me. Apart from the gunners, they'd all been to better schools

than I had, yet there I was, twenty-one years old, commanding a crew in which the navigator was an old Etonian and the rear gunner had already done a tour of ops and had a DFM. The war was a great leveler."

From the beginning of 1943, the RAF replaced the copilot in its four-engined bombers with a new flight engineer, who managed the fuel system, assisted the pilot with the engine handling, and generally acted as Mister Fix-it in the air. In the USAAF, however, the copilot was always an integral member of the crew, with the added task, in lead planes, of checking the formation from the tail turret while the lead pilot occupied his right-hand cabin seat.

Bill Ganz, who flew thirty-two missions with the 398th Bomb Group, was fully qualified to fly the B-17 but, in his time at Nuthampstead, he seldom got the chance to make a takeoff or a landing. "My pilot always wanted the takeoff. I read out the checklist and made sure he went through the standard operating procedures. It was the same with the landing. Once we got off, either he or I would fly to altitude while the other watched the instruments and after we formed up, we would split the formation time. That was the most tiring thing of all—flying formation."

The standard British bomber crew included two air gunners—one for the rear turret and one for the mid-upper—who (unlike their USAAF counterparts) received special training in deflection shooting air-to-air. Wireless operators were also trained in gunnery, and could replace an injured man in either turret if required. The front gun turret

far left below: A 388BG B-17 gunner, far left: 388BG gunners clean their .50-caliber guns at Knettishall, left: Waist gunner S/Sgt.James C. Wooden of Houston, Texas, at his position in a 385BG aircraft at Great Ashfield, below: A happy, lucky B-17 crew at the 303BG Molesworth base on returning from their final mission, June 1943.

was seldom used on normal operations—it was manned by the bomb-aimer on those rare occasions—and many pilots thought it served only to supplement the aircraft's "built-in head wind."

Eighth Air Force gunners, of whom there might be six or seven in a crew, often had a dual role, doubling as engineer, armorer, radio operator, or "toggleer"—a designation which entered the vocabulary when the Eighth developed the technique of formation bombing to a point where trained bombardiers were only needed in the lead and deputy lead crews. In an emergency, any man except the pilot might be required to fire a gun.

The rapidity with which a newly graduated USAAF pilot reached a bomber squadron contrasted sharply with the progress of his British counterpart. The American could occupy the seat of a B-17 or B-24 within weeks of being awarded his pair of silver wings; the RAF man, on the other hand, after graduation underwent further courses on twin-engine aircraft before he ever got to fly a Lancaster or Halifax. There was certainly a need for overseas-trained pilots to become adjusted to the weather, the blackout, and the enemy's proximity, but 180 flying hours spread across six months seemed more than enough, certainly for those who had been trained in America. Perhaps the British air staff had not fully realized how much more air experience the USAAF Arnold Scheme provided than the Empire schools.

"Honest John" Searby was the second-

156

tour commander of an elite RAF pathfinder squadron and a master bomber. He took the view that Bomber Command stood or fell by the quality of its navigators. "A competent, confident navigator," he wrote, "was a powerful factor for morale. Courage, determination and the will to press on in the face of flak and fighters was one thing, but only the skill of the navigator could ensure that the effort was taken to the vital spot. So much depended on him, yet we all took him for granted. He was expected to produce the answers at the drop of a hat."

At the age of twenty-one, navigator W. W. Ford of the 92nd Bomb Group was the fourth oldest member of his crew. "The engineer was twenty-six," he recalled, "the co-pilot twenty-five, and the armorer-gunner twenty-three. The aircraft commander was the youngest—he was all of nineteen—and the rest were between nineteen and twenty. We had all denominations. The pilot was a staunch bluestocking Presbyterian, we had a Jewish boy from Brooklyn, one gunner was a Mormon, the engineer was a southern Baptist, I think the tail gunner was a Methodist, the radio operator and one of the waist gunners were Catholics, the other waist gunner was a Protestant, and I was in the Episcopal church. As for the copilot, I'm sure he was at least an agnostic."

In May 1944, Keith Newhouse, by then a deputy lead pilot with the 790th Bomb Squadron, made this diary note: "We flew a practice mission and took along the navigator who has just been assigned to us. He is not operational yet, and is as green as En-

157

far left: The pilot of an RAF Stirling in 1943, left, top and bottom: Jack Woods was a Halifax wireless operator/gunner, below: Nick Kosciuk who fled Poland when the Nazis arrived and made his way to England where his pilot training in the Polish air force made it possible for him to fly Wellington bombers.

A Wellington dorsal gunner at Middleton St George, May 1943. The drawing is by Canadian official war artist Paul Goranson.

gland's rolling hills. Had him lost any number of times. It was only his second trip in a B-24, and his first time at altitude. He has lots to learn."

Navigator Sidney Rapoport arrived in England in the late summer of 1944, and was at once required to undertake a radar course. "The first thing at Alconbury," he said, "was indoctrination—you had to forget whatever you learned about navigation in the States. We started from scratch and it was a crash program." Discovering a talent for operating Mickey, Rapoport passed the course with flying colors, and was assigned to the 94th Bomb Group at Bury St. Edmunds, where he joined a pathfinder crew of the 333rd Squadron. At first, he flew practice missions every day. "We went up to 25,000 feet and made a lot of bomb runs—the library in Cambridge, Oxford University, and many other points. British radar was checking us and giving us the score. Then we would fly a mission and get a seventy-two-hour pass. That was a marvelous privilege."

Fred Allen's Halifax crew was formed during training in the customary RAF do-it-yourself way. "There were probably three hundred in the room, and you don't know who's who. You just started walking about and if you liked the look of someone: 'Have you got a gunner?' The pilot was six foot three and I thought, He can handle anything. We hit it off and that was that. Then me and another gunner talked and I said, 'I'll go in the tail if you like.' He said, 'That suits me, I'll go in the mid-upper.' We picked the engineer up at heavy conversion unit.

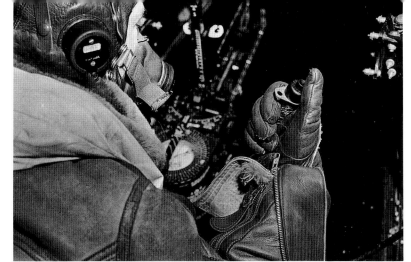

left: The bomb aimer of an RAF Lancaster, below: A Lancaster wireless operator/air gunner.

below: 385BG ball turret gunner Arnold Willingham, right: B-24 crewman dressing at Hardwick for a mission, far right: Radio operator/gunner Lloyd Stovall was part of the crew of *Bad Penny,* a 398BG B-17 at Nuthampstead, below center: 385BG tail gunner S/Sgt.G.F.Heckler, below right: navigator 2nd Lt. R.E.Bennett at the 385BG Great Ashfield base.

Thirty-eight, he was, an old man, nearly twice our age. But he knew engines, plus he played piano and he had an accordion. He was always useful and a good man with the crew."

In common with every crew who cared about survival, Allen's crewmates in *Friday the Thirteenth* were sparing in their use of the intercom. "We wouldn't say a word that wasn't absolutely necessary. We had a spare bod on board once, and he kept thinking his intercom was bust, because he couldn't hear anything. He said afterward he'd never flown with a crew that were so quiet. We thought if we kept the intercom clear, it would be there when we needed it. You didn't want to have to say, 'Oy, get off the intercom, this is important.' Too late then. Fractions of seconds counted. Maybe that's why we did thirty-eight ops and came back."

Paul Sink of the 493rd confirmed Fred Allen's view. "Usually in the airplane, it was very quiet: the only time we had much conversation was while we were under attack, calling out positions, type of aircraft, losses, or whatever. For the rest of the time the intercom was kept very clear."

With two engines giving trouble, Allen's crew once landed at a USAAF base, and he chatted with the Fortress gunners. "We wouldn't go up at night," they told him, "don't know how you can do it." Allen examined the B-17's ball turret with interest. "The gunner was a bit tight in there," he commented. "He needed somebody to help him out. We saw them come back from a trip next day and one of those ball turrets was shot away underneath. There was half a body in it. And they couldn't understand us going at night."

Although in Air Force circles the ball turret was referred to as "the morgue," statistics show that the occupant's chances of survival were slightly better than the other gunners'. For his part, Ken Stone of the 381st was content with the position: "I could turn through 360 degrees, I could go down, turn around, and go back up, so I had vision all the way around the plane. I could see everything."

Comparing it, however, with the isolation of the ball and tail turrets, and with the numbing chill of the waist positions, Larry Bird favored the toggleer's location: "There was a hot air vent in the nose, and I didn't need to wear an electric suit or any of that stuff. Sitting in the nose there, you had the most beautiful views in the world—the Swiss Alps, Lake Constance—I was in a very good spot. I didn't have to worry about the bombsight: my job was to handle that little button and keep my eye on the lead plane. As soon as I saw his bomb doors open, I'd open mine. Everybody opens in unison. So when the bombs go, they go together, and they make a pattern of explosions on the ground, same shape as the formation."

Navigator Charles Bosshardt recalled that a nose gunner's station in the B-24 was not always a healthy place to be: "We lost the hydraulics to the nose, the turret whipped around, and the doors blew off. Ernie Devries was in there holding on for dear life to keep from getting sucked out. He was a cot-

Quit yourselves like men.

—I Samuel 4:9.

"You can't slow up the formation for ten men in a crippled plane when it endangers the lives of hundreds more. The policy is to let the unfortunate drop out, so a fellow either rides the hell out of his remaining three engines and stays in, or peels off and takes a chance on getting a fighter escort back."

Keith Newhouse, pilot, 467BG

To be a member of a bomber crew required persistent fortitude at a time when the stoutest mind and heart would have every excuse to show a natural and normal weakness. The average operation was in darkness and in the early hours of the morning; every one who took part in it knew that the odds were against the survival of any particular airman.

—W. J. Lawrence, historian of No. 5 Group, RAF Bomber Command

Greater love hath no man than this, that a man lay down his life for his friends.

—John 15:13.

On October 10, 1943, then-Lieutenant Robert Rosenthal, above, piloted the only 100BG B-17 to bomb the target at Munster and then safely return to Thorpe Abbotts. On that day the 100BG lost 12 of the 14 aircraft it despatched, one having crash-landed on the airfield at Wattisham.

The great majority of the young air crew of Bomber Command never completed their first tour. That was what 4 per cent losses meant. Such was the inexorable but simple arithmetic of the strategic bombing offensive.

—from *Yesterday's Gone*, by N. J. Crisp

ton-topped kid from Roberts, Montana, about eighteen years old, and he used to call me Pa. Finally he made his plight known to me, and I used the manual crank so he could get out. After that, he felt even closer to me."

It wasn't every man who had the mental stamina to go on, mission after mission, knowing that the odds against survival were getting longer all the time. Sometimes, resolution failed, and that was not surprising. The remarkable thing was that so few combat fliers ever threw in the towel. One RAF pilot, who flew a tour of operations at a time when Bomber Command's losses were at their worst, said of such cases: "I knew of only three among the thousand men who must have come and gone in those eight months. None of us blamed them or derided them—in fact I remember someone saying, "I wish I had the guts to go LMF," and not entirely as a joke—but those three chaps were treated pretty harshly. They were sent away to some corrective establishment, they lost their rank and privileges, and their documents were labeled 'lack of moral fibre.' I expect the stigma stayed with them for life."

In the treatment of its weaker members, the RAF's posture was different from the USAAF's, which was less censorious and a great deal more humane: in the Eighth Air Force, "combat fatigue" was a condition to be recognized and treated with compassion. Larry Bird of the 493rd Bomb Group knew one crewman at Debach who decided, halfway through his second tour, that the time had come to stop. "His buddy was killed," Bird remembered, "and he just wouldn't fly

anymore. You never heard anybody say a word against him. Everybody was as friendly as they ever were." Tail gunner Paul Sink corroborated this: "I never heard of anyone who was mistreated or ostracized when he got to the point where he wouldn't fly anymore. They came into the mess hall like everyone else did. I had some good friends who got to that point, and I had a lot of sympathy with them because I knew what it was like."

The RAF practice, when a new crew joined a squadron, was to give the pilot his first experience of action by flying as "second dickey" with a seasoned crew, while his own men stayed behind, hoping they would see him back again. Some Eighth Air Force squadrons followed that procedure: on others the process of initiation was reversed. "What they did with a new crew," Bosshardt observed, "was to send them on their first mission with an experienced copilot, while their own copilot went with another crew. Our first copilot was a guy named Leo Hipp from New Jersey. The plane he went in suffered some hits and had one or two engines out. In trying to land it at the base it got out of control, and Leo and all the crew but two were killed. That made us all superstitious about flying with anyone other than our own pilot."

"The crew was very congenial," said Paul Sink. "We were very close. If a person didn't meet the expectations of the rest of the crew, he was replaced. We took classes together and spent a lot of time together. When we weren't flying, we'd go to the tower and watch the group take off. Sometimes we'd split in half, and each group would do what they wanted to do, but most of the time we were nine people together. You got to know those people very well. After you flew missions with people, especially in combat, you got to know what their reaction would be in any given circumstance."

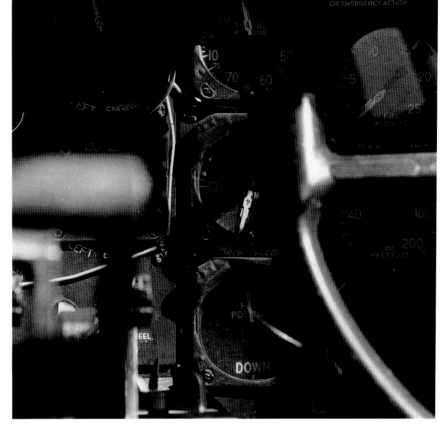

right: A detail from the cockpit panel of a B-17G,
below: 388BG pilot Richard E.Bynum, at Knettishall, April 9, 1944.

Fire tries gold, misery tries brave men.

—Seneca

JACKETS

458BG

390BG

Flamboyant artwork often decorated the fronts and backs of A2 leather flight jackets in WWII. It frequently

388BG

388BG

381BG

392BG

384BG

388BG

306BG

398BG

replicated the nose art painted on the wearer's aircraft. Pin-up girls of the Vargas variety were popular subjects. Some designs were suggestive, some lewd. Some carried threats directed at the enemy. Such decoration, while against army rules, proliferated and helped to boost aircrew morale.

THE STORY OF PEENEMÜNDE begins in April 1943, when reports of unusual enemy activity on the Baltic coast reach the British government. The photo-recce of the peninsula shows newly built laboratories, a living site, and areas that, after long consideration, the interpreters identify as missile-launching pads. It is known that German research into the atom bomb has made little progress, and that a massive effort is being put into the development of pilotless bombers and long-range rockets. In Winston Churchill's words, "Peenemünde is the summit of research and experiment."

Throughout the early summer, intelligence material about the "V-weapons" continues to accumulate. It reveals that Hitler intends to commence a bombardment of London on October 30; by the end of the year, the Führer hopes, the city will be devastated, the British will give in, and, free of invasion threats against the western seaboard, the full weight of the Wehrmacht can be thrown against the Russians. The threat is a real one, and plans to evacuate the capital, wholly or partially, are taken from the shelf where they have lain dormant since 1939.

Meanwhile, Whitehall then decides that every effort must be made to put Peenemünde out of business, and the task, codenamed *Hydra* (the many-headed snake that gave Hercules so much trouble), is assigned to Air Chief Marshal Harris. Instructions are issued from "the hole" at High Wycombe: the attack will be in strength, and in full moonlight, despite the advantage to the German fighters; the crews are not to know the

A BRITISH RAID

BY SERGEANT JACK CURRIE, NO.12 SQUADRON, RAF WICKENBY

We're on ops tonight. Target Munich . . . Quite naturally we're all very tired and moaning because it will be another trip of eight hours . . . a spoonful of pink mixture to settle my stomach, five B1 tablets to give me a bit of energy and two caffeine tablets to keep me awake, so I felt like a walking chemist's shop.

—from *Journeys into Night,* by Don Charlwood

left: The Jack Currie crew before the raid of January 14, 1944, to Brunswick, l. to r.: P/O Larry Myring, bomb aimer; Sgt. Jack Currie, pilot; F/S Len Bretell, rear gunner; Sgt. George Protheroe, mid-upper gunner; Sgt. Johnny Walker, flight engineer; Sgt. Charlie Fairbairn, wireless operator/air gunner.

nature of the target—only that this Hydra has to be eliminated, however herculean the task.

There are innovations: the bombing height band will be 8,000 to 10,000 feet—less than half the norm, a "master of ceremonies" will control events above the target for the first time in a full-scale attack, and new slow-burning "spot fires" will be used as target markers. In the late afternoon of Tuesday, August 17, almost six hundred bomber crews assemble in briefing rooms throughout the length and breadth of eastern England.

One of those crews was mine, and what follows is our story of the Peenemünde attack. We had come together in the usual random manner, responding to a call of "Sort yourselves out, chaps," in an echoing hangar at the operational training unit. Within five minutes, a bomber crew was formed: three bright Australians (the first I had met) as navigator, bomb-aimer, and rear gunner, a quiet Northumbrian as wireless operator, and me. Later, converting to the Lancaster, we had added two teenagers: a Welshman as mid-upper gunner and a Merseysider as flight engineer. At least I was no longer the youngest in the crew.

We were assigned to No. 12 Squadron—"the shiny dozen"—at Wickenby, near Lincoln, and they seemed to need us: they had lost four crews in seven days. Ahead lay a tour of thirty operations, and the chances of survival were roughly one in four; they improved, said the old hands, if you got through five missions. We did that, and another three; now we were ready for our ninth.

I had come to trust the airplane and to know the crew. Jim Cassidy, having quietly used a sick-bag as soon as we were airborne, would navigate us to Germany and back with no further trace of frailty. He had always set his heart on being a navigator, unlike many who first aspired to pilots' wings; he had come out top in training, and it showed. Larry Myring, to whom *bloody* was an all-purpose, mandatory adjective, would complain about the cold and be happy only when the target came in sight. The gunners Charlie Lanham and George Protheroe were always constantly alert; up to now, they had not been required to fire their guns in anger. Charles Fairbairn would be heard only when something urgent—a recall, a diversion, or a change of wind—came through on the radio, and Johnny Walker would do what was needed to conserve the fuel. My responsibility, as captain, was to make the big decisions—like which dance hall or cinema we went to on a stand-down night.

The *Hydra* briefing started with a little white lie. The enemy, said the intelligence officer, were developing a new generation of radar-controlled night fighters on the Baltic coast. That was the carrot. The squadron commander took over with the stick. If we failed to clobber Peenemünde tonight, we would go again the next night and the next until we did. The attack, he continued, would comprise three ten-minute waves: the first would hit the scientists' living quarters, the second wave the airfield (in reality, the

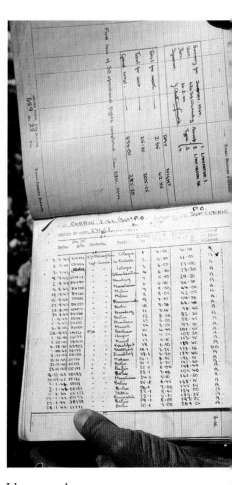

I have taught you my dear flock, for above thirty years/ how to live; and I will show you in a very short time how to die.

—Sandys

above left and right: The station armory and officers' lavatory at RAF Marston Moor, left: The Lancaster "N Nan" on completion of her 100th bombing operation in July 1944, above: Jack Currie's pilot's log book.

Having released its bombs, each aircraft was supposed to continue on the same steady course with bomb doors open until a photograph of the result was obtained. The camera in the bomb bay was triggered by flares released with the bombs. Good target photographs were not too common. The camera could be prematurely triggered by someone else's flares.

rocket-launching sites), and the third the laboratories.

"Hey, skip," Myring whispered, "what's our squadron motto?"

I glanced at him. "You know perfectly well."

"Yeah, 'Leads the field.' So how is it we're always in the last bloody wave?"

The PFF would employ the *Newhaven* method—which meant visual ground marking—and would "re-center" the markers on each successive aiming point. We were to listen out on channel "C" for the MC's instructions, and follow them to the letter. Purely as a precaution, in case the markers should be temporarily obscured, we were to approach the target on "time-and-distance" runs from Cape Arkona on Rügen Island, forty miles north of Peenemünde. The outbound route would keep us clear of known flak concentrations, and the target defenses were expected to be light. As for the enemy night fighters, they would be diverted by no less than eight Mosquitoes bothering Berlin at the time of the attack.

After the navigation leader had specified the courses, heights, and airspeeds, the weatherman performed his magic-lantern show of cloud tops and bases. "Looks good," said Cassidy. "Larry should get plenty of visual pinpoints." He looked meaningfully at the bomb-aimer, whose map-reading ability he had sometimes questioned. Myring then grunted: for him, the main business of the briefing began only when the bombing leader took the stage. He licked his pencil, and made a careful note of how his five-ton

load would be disposed.

The signals leader spoke in an apologetic undertone: "I would like to see all wireless operators for just a few minutes after briefing." I leaned across to ask Fairbairn. "What's all the secrecy, Charles? Why can't he tell everybody?"

"It's just technical stuff, Jack. A pilot wouldn't understand."

The veteran gunnery leader, with a battered service cap worn at an angle, advised constant vigilance. Defying popular belief, he saw the moonlight as being to our advantage: "A fighter will stick out like a sore thumb," he observed. "Just keep your eyes peeled and make sure you see him before he sees you."

The station commander strolled onto the stage, one hand in his pocket, the other smoothing a sleek, dark mustache. He was sure he didn't have to emphasize the importance of the target, and anxious that there should be no early returns. "Your flying meals will be ready at nineteen-thirty hours, transport to the aircraft at twenty-fifteen. Good luck, chaps."

The trouble with the Lancaster, apart from being cramped for space and deathly cold at altitude, was that it had a tendency to swing left on takeoff. If you overcorrected, it swung back to the right, and the more you tried to straighten up, the more it deviated. The trick was to eliminate the swing by leading with the throttle of the port outer engine until the speed was high enough to get the rudders in the airflow for directional control. That was what I did at thirty minutes after nine, and PH-George 2 climbed away at maximum boost and 2,850 rpm. At fields all over Lincolnshire, in Yorkshire, and in East Anglia, 595 pilots did the same. Theoretically, if every aircraft stayed within a two-mile radius of base, their climbing orbits should never coincide: in practice, they occasionally did, and we took precautions.

Apart from the navigator, busy at the gee-box, every man kept watch.

We reached 8,000 feet in under twenty minutes, and that was not too bad. Climbing in a circle wasted lift and thrust: aeroplanes climbed better in nice straight lines. When George 2 was straightened out on course she gained another 3,000 feet in the next five

The ugliest of trades have their moments of pleasure./ Now, if I were a grave-digger, or even a hangman, there are some people I could work for with a great deal of enjoyment.

—from "Ugly Trades," by Douglas Jerrold

left: Acting Group Captain John H.Searby was awarded the RAF Distinguished Service Order for his part in the Peenemunde attack of August 1943, below: A Canadian aircrew arrives at their Halifax for the evening raid.

minutes. (It was a curious convention with aircraft as with ships that, no matter how obviously masculine their names, they were always female to their crews.)

Beneath us there was nothing to be seen: the coastal crossing point at Mablethorpe did not exist as houses, streets, and shoreline, but as 53.20N 00.16E on the navigator's chart. At two minutes before ten, I switched off the navigation lights and the IFF, and George 2 headed out across the unseen waters in a straight line for "point A," seventy miles west of the North Frisian Islands.

"Skipper from mid-upper, okay to test the guns?"

"Go ahead."

The Lancaster trembled as the gunners fired short bursts from their Brownings, and the sharp smell of cordite filtered through my mask. Climbing steadily, I followed the eternal visual routine: clockwise round the panel, clockwise round the sky. "Cultivate the roving eye, Cue-ree," were the words that First Lieutenant Sena, USAAC, had constantly intoned when he was teaching me to fly the Vultee BT-13. Then, there were only "needle, ball, and airspeed" and the clear, blue sky of Georgia for the eye to rove around, but the principle held good.

I leveled out at 18,000 feet, and Walker brought the pitch back to cruising rpm. George 2 reached point A at twenty minutes after eleven. "Pilot from navigator, turn onto one-zero-seven magnetic."

"One-zero-seven. Turning on."

"I'm losing the gee signals now, but I think we're pretty well on track."

I conjured up a mental map of the Frisian Islands. "Let's try not to overfly Sylt, Jim."

"No, she'll be right, Jack. We should be well north of it."

Someone switched a mike on. With two of the crew, I knew who it was before he spoke: Myring, because his mask never seemed to keep the slipstream noises out, and Fairbairn, because he always gave two low whistles—"Phsew, phsew"—to check that he had switched from radio to intercom. This was Myring. "Can't we have the bloody heat up a bit? It's cold enough down here to freeze the balls off a brass bloody monkey."

I said, "No chatter, Larry," but I had to admit he had a point. The aircraft's fabric wore a ghostly film of frost: ice crystals sparkled on the aerials and guns. I was beating alternate hands on knees to retain some sense of touch, and was starting to lose contact with my feet.

"Wireless op, is the cabin heat on full?"

Cassidy answered for him. "He's on WT, listening out for the group broadcast."

"Tell him to turn the heat up when he's finished."

"Aw, it's pretty well up now, Jack."

"Not enough. The outside air temperature's less than minus twenty."

It was all right for Fairbairn. He sat nearest to the hot air vent. He could have flown in his underwear if he didn't have to move around the aircraft now and then. Cassidy was all right too: his navigation desk, forward of the wireless set, was never really

Plough deep while sluggards sleep.

—Benjamin Franklin

far left above: A long derelict airfield building at RAF Elvington, left above: Gooseneck flares that were often used to light the flare path at RAF airfields in WWII, center left: The signals square at RAF Binbrook, Lincolnshire, left: A hardstand that survives in the 1990s at the former RAF Bardney, near Lincoln, top: Former 10 Squadron Halifax rear gunner, Eric Barnard, above: Former 44 Squadron pilot Laurence Pilgrim.

"We were going out in daylight. Three hundred and fifty on the raid. The bomb-aimer was up front looking out. He said, 'Enemy coast coming up . . . now.' The navigator said, 'Bang on time.' I'm sitting at the back and I said, 'In that case there's three hundred and forty-nine other buggers late, 'cause I can see them fifty miles behind us.' "I'd no sooner said that, than 'boom, boom,' and the shells burst just behind me. They were getting closer. I said, 'Dive port,' and the skipper turned and dived straight away. Just as well, because the next one burst exactly where I'd been. It blew the perspex off the turret. Cut me eye and me thumb a bit as well."

Fred Allen, rear gunner, 158 Sqn.

The night is dark, and I am far from home.

—from "Lead, Kindly Light," by John Henry Newman

right: Air Vice Marshal Donald Bennett helped change the course of the war when he became commander of the RAF Pathfinder Force which turned the uneven performance of RAF Bomber Command raids into one of the decisive factors in the defeat of Germany.

cold. Walker and I, farther forward in the cabin, were only ever warm when we were flying at low altitude on a summer's day, and Myring's station in the nose was colder than a tax collector's heart.

"Pilot from navigator, enemy coast coming up in two minutes."

"Roger. Let's have an intercom check. Bomb-aimer?"

"Loud and clear, skip."

"Wireless op?"

"Phsew, phsew. Strength five."

"Mid-upper . . ."

At eleven-fifteen, the moon showed its head above the northeastern horizon. Myring, mindful of the navigator's hint, came through on the intercom. "Bomb-aimer, Jim. We're crossing the coast now—fairly well on track."

"I need it exactly, Larry."

"Oh, yeah. Well, about fifteen miles south of Esbjerg, or whatever they call the bloody place."

"Lat and long, Larry, and the time."

"Christ, Jim. It's not that easy down here, trying to use me bloody torch an' look at the bloody map, and—"

I cut in. "Do your best, bomb-aimer."

As George 2 headed east-southeast across the southern plains of Denmark, Lanham called from the rear turret: "Flak astern of us, ten degrees to starboard."

"Roger." Some airmen behind us were a little south of track, and the guns of Sylt were making them aware of it.

Walker checked the fuel. George 2 was half a ton lighter than her takeoff weight.

"Let's reduce the revs a bit," I suggested. "We should be able to maintain airspeed at twenty-three hundred."

Walker inched the levers down, and I turned the elevator trim minutely back. George 2 reacted badly to the trivial economy. Her indicated airspeed fell by nearly five miles per hour, and she handled like a ship without a rudder.

"No go, Johnny, try twenty-three-fifty."

Ten minutes passed while we struggled to regain George 2's goodwill. Five minutes before midnight, Myring came through with a pinpoint; ten minutes later he produced another. "Fifty-four forty-eight north, twelve thirty-nine east, time . . . er, bloody hell . . . zero-zero-zero-five."

"Good on yer, Larry," said Cassidy.

I began a gradual descent to the bombing height as George 2 crossed the southern Swedish islands and continued east-southeast. The moonlight showed the shapes of other bombers, well scattered, moving like a ghostly skein of geese across the Baltic Sea.

"The wind's picked up a bit," said the navigator. "We'll be early at point C. Can you reduce the speed?"

"Can't go much slower than one-fifty, Jim. I can make an orbit—how much time do you want to lose?"

"Three minutes ought to do it."

It was not a maneuver I would have cared to make in total darkness or in cloud but, in the moonlight, it was not too hazardous. While the crew watched out, George 2 completed a wide descending circle without bumping into any other aeroplanes. Shortly

174

before we reached the turning point at Cape Arkona, Myring saw the first green spot fires burning on Peenemünde. The time was seventeen minutes after midnight, and we had fifty miles to run.

The last wind velocity Cassidy had found was from 290 degrees at forty miles per hour; Myring fed the numbers into the bombsight's calculator. Now the curve of the coast was perfectly distinct, and a white line of surf showed on the shore. The scene ahead was much less serene. The detonating "cookies" made bright, expanding circles, like heavy stones dropped into pools of liquid fire; searchlights were waving, flak bursts were twinkling, and fires were taking hold. Not so many searchlights, nor so much flak as we were accustomed to, but a lot of smoke—more than the fires would seem to justify. The people on Peenemünde were putting up a smoke screen. It was a nice try, and it might have been successful—if the wind hadn't blown it out to sea.

From 9,000 feet, in the light of the full moon, the target was much closer, and warmer, than the norm. I told Fairbairn to reduce the cabin heat, and Walker turned the oxygen to "high." On the starboard beam an interlacing pattern of tracer bullets appeared and disappeared. The voice of the MC sounded on the radio, the cool, clear voice of someone accustomed to command. It was strange, and rather comforting, to hear that English voice in the headphones, high above the Baltic, six hundred miles from home. "Come in, third wave, and bomb the center of the green TIs. Let's have a good

concentration. Aim right at the center of the greens."

"Switches on," said Myring, in the special, growling tone he adopted for the moment—his moment of all moments. "Bombs fused and selected."

I took a deep breath and a fresh grip on the wheel. A spatter of light flak danced around George 2: I tried to pretend it wasn't there. "Running in nicely, skip," said Myring, "steady as she goes."

"Third wave, don't bomb short. Make sure you aim at the center of the greens." I turned down the volume; from now on Myring was in charge.

"Bomb doors open, skip."

I pushed the lever. The roar of the slipstream made a deeper sound as the bomb bay gaped. George 2 tried to raise her nose, and I stilled her with the trim tab. "Lanc on fire at four o'clock level," said Lanham. "It's going down."

"Steady," Myring growled, "left, left . . . steady, steady . . . a touch left, and steady . . . steady . . . bombs gone!"

Down went the 4,000-pound cookie, six 1,000-pounders and the two 500-pounders. George 2 lifted as they fell. Cassidy logged the time: thirty-eight minutes after midnight. "Bomb doors closed," called Myring. "Steady for the camera." In the last few minutes he had uttered thirty words without a single *bloody*. He really was a changed man with a bomb-tit in his hand.

"Bomb doors closed," I echoed, pulling up the lever and rolling back the trim. Thirty seconds passed while the photo plates ticked

. . . Ferris groped under his heated flying suit, and touched the hard shape of the silver plated cigarette case which he had slipped into the left-hand breast pocket of his battledress, a final check that it was actually there. The cigarette case was a birthday present, and Ferris never used it. He only ever carried it when he flew on operations. One of these days, it might serve to deflect a shell fragment from his heart. You never knew.

—from *Yesterday's Gone*, by N. J. Crisp

right: A Frank Wootton painting of a Blenheim raid.

over, and before I turned George 2 away, away from the brightly burning debris that was Peenemünde. "New course, nav?"

"Two-nine-five degrees magnetic."

"Turning on. Give me twenty-eight-fifty, Johnny, and we'll grab some altitude."

George 2 climbed away smoothly and headed to the west. We had no way of knowing that the Nachtjagd controllers, aware now that the Berlin raid was no more than a feint, had redirected all their available Messerschmitts and Junkers to our homeward route.

The Lancaster's electronics included a receiver that picked up transmissions from the Lichtenstein radar sets in the German fighters. The radar device was code-named *Boozer*, perhaps because the red lamp it lighted on the panel was reminiscent of a heavy drinker's nose. At 18,000 feet over Stralsund, thirty miles west of Peenemünde, the roving eye picked the glow up straight away.

"Rear gunner from pilot, I have a *Boozer* warning."

"Rear gunner watching out astern."

Boozer also read transmissions from the ground-based *Würzburg* radars, which could be quite a nuisance when you were flying in the stream; at all times, however, you had to heed the signal. It was as well we did: seconds later, Lanham spoke again. "Fighter at seven o'clock low. Stand by to corkscrew."

"Standing by."

"Mid-upper from rear gunner. There could be a pair. I'll take care of this one, you

watch out."

I didn't like the sound of that remark. It would be difficult enough to evade one fighter in the moonlight, let alone two. I sat up straight, and gently shook the wheel. Don't get excited, George 2, but you might be doing some aerobatics any minute now.

"Prepare to corkscrew port, Jack . . . corkscrew port . . . go!"

"Going port."

I used heavy left aileron and rudder, elevators down, held the diving turn through fifteen degrees, I pulled out sharply, and turned hard to starboard halfway through a climb. George 2 responded like a PT-17—a PT-17 weighing twenty-five tons.

"Foxed him, Jack. He's holding off, level on the starboard quarter."

Protheroe then came through. "Another bandit, skipper, four o'clock high, six hundred yards. It's an Me 210 . . ."

Lanham broke in. "Watch him, George, here comes number one again. Corkscrew starboard . . . go!"

According to the navigator's log, the combat continued for another eight minutes: to me it seemed longer. After each frustrated pass, the attacker held off, content to occupy the attention of one gunner, while his partner came on in. I longed to have the heat turned down—the sweat was running down my face—but I dared not interrupt the gunners' running commentary. The sound of heavy breathing was sufficiently distracting, and I knew that it was mine.

My wrists and forearms were reasonably strong, but I was no Charles Atlas, and

George 2 wasn't feeling like a Stearman anymore. It occurred to me that these two fighter pilots were just playing games with us, biding their time until I was exhausted. Then they would rip the Lancaster to shreds. The sheet of armor plate behind me seemed pitifully small, and there was a lot of me it failed to shield. If only our Brownings had a greater range; if only I could find a layer of cloud to hide in; if only the moonlight wasn't quite so bright . . .

"Corkscrew port . . . go!"

Throwing George 2 into another diving turn, I looked back through the window. There was the Messerschmitt again, turning steeply with me as the pilot tried to bring his guns to bear. I could see his helmet and his goggles, looking straight at me. Staring back at him, I felt a sudden surge of anger, and a change of mood. You're not good enough, Jerry, I thought, to win this little fight. You're a bloody awful pilot and a damn poor shot. "Well, for Christ's sake, George," I squawked into the microphone, "shoot that bastard down."

Instantly, the Lancaster vibrated. At first the flashes dazzled me, but when Protheroe fired a second burst I saw the streams of tracer make a sunbright parabola between George 2 and the fighter's nose. The Messerschmitt rolled over and went down. The last I saw of that bloody awful pilot was a long trail of smoke, ending in the stratus far below.

"I think you got him," I said. "Where's the other one?"

"Falling back astern," said Lanham.

"He's clearing off. Probably out of ammo or fuel."

"Good shooting, George. What kept you?"

"Sorry, skipper. I had my sights on him all the time. I guess I just forgot to pull the trigger."

"Pilot from nav, let me know when you're back on course."

"Roger."

"Bomb-aimer, skip. I was ready for the buggers, but they never came in bloody range of the front bloody guns . . ."

Larry was himself again. I checked the compass, and turned toward the coast of Lübeck Bay. I was thinking of the Welshman, sitting in the turret with the fighter in his sights. He had fired a lot of rounds on training ranges and at air-towed target drogues, but he had never fired a bullet at another human being. That was rather different, and I thought I understood why he had needed the command to open fire.

"Nav from pilot, back on course. Let's all settle down."

I held the wheel loosely, and stroked the rudder pedals with the balls of my feet. George 2 was flying head-on into wind, and her speed across the water was a mere 176 mph. It was going to be a long ride back to Wickenby, but I believed that we would make it. At twenty minutes after one, Lanham reported in that the Peenemünde fires could still be seen.

Forty-three minutes later, a searchlight reared ahead, pale in the moonlight but no less dangerous for that. I really hated search-

Germany heard a clashing of arms all over the sky; the Alps trembled with uncommon earthquakes. . . . Never did lightnings fall in greater quantity from a serene sky, or dire thunders blaze so often.

Virgil, *Georgics*, circa 30 B.C.

They have sown the wind, and they shall reap the whirlwind.

—Hosea 8:7.

The 'cookie' somewhat resembled a giant dustbin. It had no ballistic characteristics. Once released, it could land anywhere within a five-mile radius of the aiming point.

—from *Yesterday's Gone*, by N. J. Crisp

above left: Strange light patterns in the sky over Hamburg when the shipyards there were attacked by RAF Lancasters on the night of January 30, 1943. above right: RAF officers await returning bombers from the great Nuremberg raid of March 30-31, 1944. left: A still from the film 'The Dambusters' in which Richard Todd, right, played the part of W/C Guy Gibson and Robert Shaw, left, played Sgt.Pulford, Gibson's flight engineer.

179

PEENEMÜNDE 1
nr. WOLGAST
EXPERIMENTAL ESTAB.
K 2716 (SUPP)

lights. Over the target, you just had to ignore them, but I did my best to dodge them when we were on our own. If that master beam latched on, its two slaves would quickly follow, and few aircraft, once coned, returned to base unscathed. On the way home from Hamburg, two weeks earlier, we had got away with it—more by luck than judgment. I didn't want to try our luck again. "Going ten degrees starboard for two minutes, Jim." The beam waved toward us, like a finger feeling for a keyhole in the dark; it groped for a while and then disappeared. Back on course, George 2 began her second crossing of the cold North Sea.

Just after three o'clock, the gee-box showed its first good signals since they faded at point A four hours ago. Cassidy plotted the position. For close on a thousand miles, by dead reckoning, a bearing on Polaris, and three or four pinpoints, he had navigated George 2 to within a mile of where she ought to be. He gave no sign of being surprised. "Pilot from nav, we're pretty well on track. ETA base is zero-four-zero-five."

I liked the sound of that: now the journey could be thought of in terms of minutes, not of hours. I could begin the descent, engage the autopilot, and drink a cup of coffee. I might even struggle back to the Elsan for a piddle.

Walker reduced the rpm. The vertical speed indicator showed a descent rate of three hundred feet a minute: if I maintained that flight path, we should arrive over Wickenby more or less at circuit height and all set for a landing. Provided I remembered to lower the undercarriage, nothing then could keep us from breakfast or from bed. Not that the gunners could relax: there could be no worse anticlimax than to get chopped by an intruder in the airfield circuit.

"Pilot to crew, we're below oxygen height. Smoke if you can afford it."

At about four o'clock, the Mablethorpe searchlight stood erect, the only searchlight I was ever glad to see. I switched on the navigation lights and the IFF, and Fairbairn stood ready with the colors of the day. Ten minutes later, a beacon twinkled dead ahead. It read "dit-dit-dah-dah dit-dit"—the code for Wickenby. I told Walker to turn the oxygen up to the 20,000-feet level, and pushed the RT button "A." "Hello, Orand, this is Nemo George 2, are you receiving me, over?"

"Hello, Nemo George 2, this is Orand. Receiving you loud and clear, over."

"Orand, George 2 approaching from the east, fifteen-hundred feet. Permission to join the circuit, over."

"George 2, the circuit is busy. You're clear to join at four thousand and stand by. Left-hand orbit, two aircraft at that height, over."

"Shit," said Walker, "we're in the flipping stack."

"Yeah," snarled Myring, "that's the bloody snag with being in the last bloody wave."

"Shut up," I counseled. "It's a lovely night for flying. Twenty-eight-fifty RPM, engineer."

For the next thirty minutes, George 2

left: Peenemunde, the German V-weapons development and experimental station and target of the RAF raid of August 17-18, 1943, below: A former bomb aimer with 51 Squadron, Tony Partridge.

"We arrived at Snaith, and had an interview with the CO. He said, 'Don't worry, we'll start you off on something easy.' Two nights later, we were on Berlin, and we went there five times in the next two weeks."

Tony Partridge, bomb-aimer, 51 Sqn.

orbited the beacon, gradually descending in five-hundred-foot stages at Orand's command. Later in the tour, I would learn to take some shortcuts, to make a better speed, and to arrive at Wickenby before the stack began, but in those days, a green sergeant pilot, I didn't know the score. At last the call came through: "George 2, you're cleared to one thousand feet and number two to land. Runway two-seven, Queenie-Fox-Easy one-zero-one-two. Call downwind, over."

I set the altimeter, and began the landing drill. "Trailing aerial in, Charles. Brake pressure, Johnny? Fuel?"

"Plenty of both."

"Rad Shutters open. Check 'M' gear."

At 1,000 feet, a mile south of the field, I turned parallel with the twin lines of the runway lights, and reduced the power.

"Orand, George 2 downwind, over."

"George 2, you're clear to funnels, one ahead."

"Wheels down, Johnny."

The undercarriage lamps shone red as the up locks disengaged, and the nose dropped a fraction as the airflow hit the wheels. The locks engaged with a jolt, and the lamps turned to green. "Flap fifteen. Booster pumps on."

When the last set of lights at the runway's downwind end were level with the port wing tip, I brought the airspeed back to 140 and turned toward the field. Halfway through the turn, the funnel lights on the port quarter beckoned like the gates of home. As the nose swung into line, I inched the throttles back and let Sir Isaac Newton

do his stuff. "George 2 funnels, over."

"George 2, you're clear to land. Wind is eighteen degrees from your right at ten knots, over."

"Half flap, Johnny. Pitch fully fine."

I held the nose down to counteract the lift and steered a mite to starboard to compensate for drift. The lights of the runway seemed to widen at the threshold and to taper in the distance up ahead. "Full flap. Stand by for landing."

As George 2 crabbed across the threshold, Walker held the throttles back against the stops, I kicked the nose straight and pulled the wheel into my lap. The tires squealed on the tarmac at 04:49.

The record showed that 560 aircraft reached the target and dropped 1,800 tons of bombs, 85 percent of which were high explosive. When the truth was revealed about the Baltic base, it was said that *Hydra* set the V-weapon program back by several months and reduced the scale of the eventual attack. Certainly, no flying bombs fell on England until June 1944, and no rockets until the following September. General Dwight D. Eisenhower was to write later: "If the Germans had succeeded in perfecting and using these new weapons six months earlier our invasion of Europe would have proved exceedingly difficult, perhaps impossible."

One hundred and eighty Germans, mostly scientists and technicians, died in the attack, and General Jeschonnek, the Luftwaffe Chief of Staff, gave proof of his dismay by committing suicide the next day. Sadly,

the first *Newhaven* markers went down on the camp where the slave workers were sleeping, and over five hundred unhappy lives were lost.

The Nachtjagd, it transpired, had deployed a new device: twin upward-firing cannons, mounted behind the cockpit of the Me 110s and fired by the pilot with the aid of a reflector sight, enabled the fighter crew to attack the bomber's blind spot underneath the fuselage. This deadly piece of weaponry, known as *Schräge Musik*, was believed to have inflicted some of the losses suffered on the night: twenty-three Lancasters, fifteen Halifaxes, two Stirlings, and one of the Mosquitoes.

For the future, an airborne MC or master bomber (the role of "Honest John" Searby, 83 Squadron's commander, over Peenemünde), would control all major raids, and the innovative tactics for "re-centering" ground markers were to be retained. Peenemünde would be the target for three Eighth Air Force missions in July and August 1944, but *Hydra* was, and would remain, the RAF's only full-scale precision attack in the last two years of the war.

Knowing nothing of these matters, we drank our cocoa with a tot of rum and attended the debriefing. The crew were in good spirits: we had hit a vital target, dodged the searchlights and the flak, outflown one Messerschmitt and destroyed another—well, possibly destroyed. It seemed a shame to remind them, as we ate our eggs and bacon, that we hadn't yet completed one third of our tour.

"Your target tonight is in Dresden. It is being used by the Germans as a railhead for the transport of men, equipment, and supplies to the Eastern Front. Our aim is to give practical help to our Russian allies by destroying the marshalling yards."

Briefing officer at RAF North Killinghome, February 13, 1945

"You may be interested to know that the flak guns in Berlin are being fired by fifteen-year-old boys as fast as Russian POWs can load them."

Briefing officer, RAF Wickenby, November 1943

Armed with a great sword, Hercules succeeded in cutting off one of the Hydra's seven heads; but he had no sooner done so than, to his dismay, he saw seven other heads spring from the bleeding stump.

The Myths of Greece and Rome, Harrap

above left: A fine aerial view of a Lancaster III in 1944, below left: Night bomber aircrew after a raid on a Nazi target.

IN RECENT YEARS, parachuting has become a popular activity. From all sorts of altitudes, in free fall or with static lines, in teams or individually, people jump out of airplanes for fun. But jumping out because you had to—because there was no alternative—was never any fun. In the great air offensive of World War II, many thousands of young men took that obligatory step into the sky, trusting slender silk and fiber to bear them safely down. And that was only the start of their adventure: there were no clubmates applauding the descent, no friendly sponsor offering a prize, but an alien environment, with the enemy in charge, and perhaps a population who bore them no goodwill. Their duty, they were told, lay in evasion and escape: bury your parachute, remove all distinguishing badges, lie low in daylight, and travel by night; make contact with the underground, try to reach a neutral country, find your way back to your squadron, and resume the fight . . .

Although the 379th Bomb Group lost fifteen B-17s in its first month in combat, it went on to fly more sorties, drop more bombs on target, and have fewer turn-backs than any other bomb group in the Eighth. (The fact that it also had more cases of VD suggests that the group pursued pleasure as vigorously as business, if rather less selectively.) On August 16, 1943, a day before the first historic Schweinfurt raid, twenty-one aircraft of the 379th took part in an attack on a fighter airfield at Le Bourget. Albert Tyler, a twenty-nine-year-old from California, was flying his fourteenth mission as top turret gunner and flight engineer. The crew's regular pilot had recently been killed, and this was to be the copilot's first combat mission in command.

The formation was flying in the height-band between 26,000 and 28,000 feet when the German fighters came at it head-on. Tyler never blamed the pilot for what happened next: "He was a helluva nice guy and we all liked him, but I guess he panicked. He did a real no-no. He pulled back on the stick and drove right up. We were on our own up there, with no protection from the other B-17s. We were sitting ducks."

Methodically, pairs of the fighters destroyed the lone aircraft, raking it with cannon fire from nose to tail. In the cabin, the hydraulic reservoir exploded, and some of the shattered metal lodged in Tyler's leg. The oxygen bottles were the next to go. Combustion quickly followed and the cabin filled with flame. The canvas cover of Tyler's parachute was burning as he clipped it on his harness. Observing that the pilot and copilot had already left the airplane ("Another no-no," Tyler commented), he took it on himself to give the order to abandon, and helped the bombardier and navigator to make their escape.

"I went out of the open bomb bay doors. Jumping from that height, I should have delayed pulling the rip cord, but I didn't want to take a chance on the chute catching fire, so I pulled it immediately. I passed out from lack of oxygen, but it could only have been seconds before I came to again."

ABANDON!

left: A crippled Liberator crosses Austria with an engine fire and a low probability of survival.

William Henry ("Buster") Prout / Stopped some flak and, baling out, / Landed safe but somewhat shaken North of Schnitzel-unter-Laken.

With what courage he could muster/ The aforesaid William ("Buster") Faced and even cracked a joke With the untersucher bloke.

(In case you do not Sprechen Deutsch,/ He's the guy whose soothing voice/ Interrogates the P.O.W.—/ Here's hoping that he'll never trouble you.)

Well, anyway, our hero found/ Himself with several such around. Good types, they seemed,—quite decent chaps,/ Who gave him fags and lots of Schnaps.

They didn't seem to ask him much,/ Just "How are all at home?" and such. Gin followed brandy, then came port. Our Buster talked— without a thought.

He didn't tell 'em much, it's true/—Just all he knew, or thought he knew. All this was noted in a file./ (He'd underrated Jerry's guile.)

Results: Some things were added to/ The store of stuff that Jerry knew. And (Buster being such a *duffer*)/ *His* pals will be the ones to suffer.

—"Just All He Knew," from *Tee Emm*

GERMAN CAMPS AND HOSPITALS WHERE AMERICAN AND BRITISH P.O.W.S WERE DETAINED

PRISONER OF WAR CAMPS
STALAG IIA/NEUBRANDENBURG
STALAG IIB/HAMMERSTEIN
STALAG IIIA/LUCKENWALDE
STALAG IIIB/FURSTENBURG/ODER
STALAG IIIC/ALTDREWITZ
STALAG IIID/BERLIN/STEGLITZ
STALAG IVA/HOHNSTEIN
STALAG IVB/MUHLBERG
STALAG IVC/WISTRITZ
STALAG IVD/TORGAU
STALAG IVD/Z/ANNABURG
STALAG IVF/HARTMANNSDORF
STALAG IVG/OSCHATZ
STALAG VA/LUDWIGSBURG
STALAG VB/VILLINGEN
STALAG VIG/BERGISCH-NEUSTADT
STALAG VIJ/KREFELD
STALAG VIIA/MOOSBURG
STALAG VIIB/MEMMINGEN
STALAG VIIIB/TESCHEN
STALAG 344/LAMSDORF
STALAG VIIIC/SAGAN
STALAG IXB/BAD ORB
STALAG IXC/BAD SULZA
STALAG XB/BREMERVORDE
STALAG XC/NIENBURG
STALAG XIA/ALTENGRABOW

STALAG XIB/FALLINGBOSTEL
STALAG XIIA/LIMBURG
STALAG XIID/WAHBREITBACH
STALAG XIIF/FREINSHEIM
STALAG XIIIC/HAMMELBURG
STALAG XIIID/NURNBERG
STALAG 383/HOHENFELS
STALAG XVIIA/KAISERSTEINBRUCH
STALAG 398/PUPPING
STALAG XVIIIA/WOLFSBERG
STALAG XVIIIC/MARKT-PONGAU
STALAG 357/OERBKE
STALAG XXA/TORUN
STALAG XXB/MARIENBURG
WK8-BAB 21/BLECHHAMMER
NAVAL CAMP
MARLAG-MILAG/TARMSTEDT
GROUND FORCE OFFICERS' CAMPS
OFLAG VIC/COLDITZ
OFLAG VIIB/EICHSTATT
OFLAG IXA/H/SPANGENBURG
OFLAG IXA/Z/ROTENBURG
CAMPS FOR AIRMEN
LUFT I/BARTH
LUFT III/SAGAN
LUFT IV/GROSSTYCHOW
STALAG XVIIB/KREMS
DULAG LUFT/WETZLAR

OFLAG XI(79)/BRUNSWICK
LUFT VII/BANKAU
OFLAG 64/ALTBURGUND
OFLAG XB/NIENBURG
HOSPITALS
IVA/RES.LAZ.ELSTERHORST
IVG/LEIPZIG
VB/ROTTENMUNSTER
VIC/RES.LAZ/LINGEN
VIG/RES.LAZ. GERRESHEIM
VIIA/FREISING
IXB/BAD SODEN/SALMUNSTER
IXC/OBERMASSFELD
IXC/MEININGEN
IXC/HILDBURGHAUSEN
XA/RES.LAZ. II, SCHLESWIG
XB/SANDBOSTEL
XIIID/NURNBERG/LANGWASSER
MARINE LAZARETT CUXHAVEN
LUFTWAFFEN LAZARETT 4/II WISMAR
RES. LAZ. II VIENNA
RES. LAZ. GRAZ
RES. LAZ. BILIN
RES. LAZ. WOLLSTEIN
RES. LAZ. II STARGARD
RES. LAZ. SCHMORKAU
RES. LAZ. KONIGSWARTHA
RES. LAZ. EBELSBACH

Two FW 190s made passes as Tyler floated down and, at a lower altitude, an Me 109 banked vertically around him. Tyler put his hand up in a gesture of salute; the enemy pilot did the same. Below him, he saw a stretch of forest and the shining river Oise; in the fields between were German trucks and soldiers. He was a good swimmer, and he tried to steer his chute toward the water, but in common with most airmen he had received no training in maneuvering a parachute. "I pulled the lines the wrong way, and I ended up in the tallest tree, right on the banks of that river. There were no Germans down there that I could see. In fact, I didn't see anybody for a while. Then a dog started barking, and a group of people gathered under the tree. With my leg the way it was, I couldn't get down."

Once they were convinced that Tyler was American, the Frenchmen dispersed, taking a fallen flying boot as a souvenir. Then a sturdy youth, whom Tyler came to know as André, climbed the tree, half held and half dropped the airman to the ground, and concealed him in a pile of rocks. A few hours later, Tyler heard someone whistling "Yankee Doodle," and two small children came through the forest carrying a basket of bread, cheese, wine, and fruit. Having improvised a crutch, André found garments suited to the role of peasant which Tyler, for the moment, would adopt.

That night, resting in a hayloft, they heard shouts of *Achtung, Achtung,* as German soldiers searched the neighborhood. Next morning, they moved to a cave beside the river, where they were joined by one of Tyler's crew, escorted by the village mayor. Tyler was troubled: "Johnny was not our regular bombardier, and he was a very un-cooperative guy. I thought he would be a real danger to me."

After the airmen had spent three nervous days in the cave, André returned with rail tickets for Paris. Although the train was thronged with soldiers, they paid no attention to the Americans, and Tyler was not called upon to use the deaf-and-dumb act he had rehearsed with André. In the Gare du Nord's urinal, Tyler and Johnny exchanged a word or two in English. "A German officer came out of a cubicle," said Tyler, "and put a pistol up against my kidneys. André hadn't said a word. He came over and jammed a hunting knife into the German's back. He said *"Allez, allez,"* and we left in a hurry."

André took his charges to the apartment of a doughty female member of the French Resistance. "There was a big, open courtyard, and our bedrooms were right off a balcony that went round the house. Madame gave us everything we wanted to eat and drink. At the same time she was hiding and feeding a bunch of escaped French POWs. A very brave lady."

Meanwhile, the Resistance were planning the next move, which was almost a disaster. In a Paris suburb, they had to jump from a window in the middle of the night to evade a German search party. Their next port of call was a fine town house a mile or two from the Eiffel Tower, and the two weeks they spent there were the high spot of their stay in France.

"Every day," said Tyler, "Juliette surprised us with something—a duck, a lobster,

above right: Albert Tyler at Kimbolton in 1943.

STANDARD TIME INDICATED
AT
Central Air Terminal
Glendale, Calif.

(32)

Postal Telegraph

Mackay Radio · All America Cables · Canadian Pacific Telegraphs

THIS IS A FULL RATE TELEGRAM, CABLE-GRAM OR RADIOGRAM UNLESS OTHERWISE INDICATED BY SYMBOL IN THE PREAMBLE OR IN THE ADDRESS OF THE MESSAGE. SYMBOLS DESIGNATING SERVICE SELECTED ARE OUTLINED IN THE COMPANYS TARIFFS ON HAND AT EACH OFFICE AND ON FILE WITH REGULATORY AUTHORITIES.

AUG 25 PM 4 54

S-NB361   N-WC318

LA348W (TWO) 40GOVT= PXXWMU WASHINGTON DC 25 538P=

MRS MYRTIS P TYLER=

16 MANNING ST (BURBANK CALIF)=

REGRET TO INFORM YOU REPORT RECEIVED STATES YOUR SON
TECHNICAL SERGEANT ALBERT P TYLER MISSING IN ACTION IN
EUROPEAN AREA SINCE SIXTEEN AUGUST IF FURTHER DETAILS OR OTHER
INFORMATION OF HIS STATUS ARE RECEIVED YOU WILL BE PROMPTLY
NOTIFIED=

    JL10 THE ADJUTANT GENERAL-==:

FOR VICTORY
BUY
UNITED
STATES
WAR
SAVINGS
BONDS
STAMPS

PIN NOT TO BE REMOVED UNTIL FUZE IS ABOUT TO BE PLACED IN BOMB. IF FUZE IS REMOVED FROM BOMB REPLACE PIN AT ONCE.

and I mean a big one. It was very enjoyable. Her husband got a big kick taking us for a stroll around the sidewalk cafés in the afternoon. The trouble was that when the Germans saw Johnny's blond hair, they thought he was one of them, and tried to strike up a conversation. He could have been picked up real quick. I suggested shoe polish, but he didn't want his hair blacked. That guy fought us tooth and nail. I had to hold him down."

They accompanied Marcel, a saboteur, on a journey south of Paris, and watched him lay explosives on a railway line that carried German traffic. Later, they saw him choke a sentry with a length of piano wire. "He wanted us," said Tyler, "to tell the English what the French Resistance were doing to help themselves."

Two days before the time came to move on, they saw barrage balloons rising over Paris, and watched from Juliette's patio while B-17s bombed the Renault engine plant across the Seine. On the train to central France, they were escorted by a priest. Arriving in Ville, they were welcomed by the mayor, who promptly threw a party. The whole town attended, much champagne was drunk, and Tyler, not America's most accomplished pianist, played the "Marseillaise" fortissimo until the more cautious townsmen persuaded him to stop.

Their next stay was at a castle on a hilltop where, over a bottle of Jack Daniel's, they discovered that their host, having made an illicit booze fortune in the States, was making amends to society by collecting

188

starving children from the poorer parts of Paris and fattening them on the products of his land. "He and his beautiful wife," said Tyler, "would take them back to town and pick up another load. That guy was some character."

Their priestly guide then left them, with instructions to take a certain train to Toulouse. In the compartment, Tyler's deaf-and-dumb act was successful until a stout lady, in rising to depart, happened to tread upon his foot. Tyler yelped, "Oh, shit," at which two Frenchmen got up from their seats, muttering, "*Allez, allez,*" and hustled the Americans away.

They were taken to a farmhouse below the northern foothills of the towering Pyrenees. That afternoon, with twenty more evaders and a guide, they set out to make a crossing into Spain. On the third day of the journey, they were halted by a blizzard, and their guide decamped, not only with his fee but with the party's store of food. While some men elected to continue on their own, Tyler and Johnny returned to the farmhouse for reprovisioning. Their next attempt to reach a neutral haven was eventually successful, but not without its hardships.

"We were eating leaves and grass," said Tyler, "to supplement our rations. I ended up with a diarrhea you wouldn't believe. And they told me, 'We can't stop, we have to go on.' The Germans were patrolling those mountain trails with light aircraft."

At last they reached Andorra, a neutral, if venal, sanctuary. It took Tyler's check for two hundred dollars, written on scrap paper,

to purchase travel documents and a passage to Madrid. From the Spanish capital, the British vice-consul drove them to Gibraltar, and an RAF transport did the rest. "They put us in a hotel in London," said Tyler, "and squeezed every bit of information out of us. The second night there, I got deathly ill. The doctor said I'd eaten too many little Spanish pastries."

On the night of October 22, 1944, Kassel was the target for a heavy attack by the RAF's bombers. Jack Woods was flying his fifteenth mission as the wireless operator of a Halifax crew. "Our aircraft was hit by flak," he recorded, "a few minutes after we bombed the target. It must have hit something vital, because the order to bail out came within seconds. The navigator opened the nose hatch, and he and the bomb-aimer jumped out. Somebody else went out before me; I think it must have been the second pilot—a new chap on his first trip. I felt the pack hit me in the face when I jumped, as it was bound to with the chest-type chutes, and I might have been dazed, because I only seemed to be in the air for a few seconds before I landed, close by a railway line. When I took the chute off I saw blood dripping on the silk— I'd got a few cuts when we were hit. I stuffed the chute in a hedge and started to walk along the line. I ought to have hidden for a while and made a plan, but I didn't think it out well enough. I didn't know whether it was Christmas or Easter, actually. I just went on walking until the Germans picked me up—railway workers, they were.

O, call back yesterday, bid time return.

—from *Richard II*, Act III, Sc. 2, by William Shakespeare

above left: The numbing phrases of a typical war department telegram in WWII, below left: A bomb cotter pin and tag from an aircraft in which Albert Tyler flew a mission in August 1943, below: Albert Tyler (at right) in 1990.

"Over Germany, they were hit in the glycol tank, just in front of Dougie's position. The tank ignited, and the flames came back toward him. He wasn't burned or anything, but it drove him back and the aircraft was all over the place. Dougie thought, 'This is it, I'm getting out,' and he jumped. He landed, stowed his parachute, and hid in a wood. Next morning, he was making his way around some hillocks and there were these German soldiers with their guns trained on him. They rounded him up and marched him through a village, where some of the people spat at him. They stuck him in the local prison with some Russian POWs. There was no food, and the Germans treated the Russians terribly, but they didn't mistreat Dougie. There was a fairly decent spirit, so long as you didn't get into the hands of the

"They took me to a work unit—Russian POWs and others—and I asked for a doctor. What I got was a crowd of Hitler Youth. They were pretty obnoxious. Next day the Luftwaffe came along and they looked after me for a couple of days before taking me to the Dulag Luft, where I was interrogated and then sent to hospital. I met some Americans there who had been shot down on Schweinfurt. Next stop was Stalag Luft IVB. It was a multinational camp, with different compounds for Russians, French, Italians, and so on. I was in the RAF compound—all flying chaps and airborne troops.

"Life was drab, and the food was pretty grim. We looked forward to the Red Cross parcels. In the American parcels, you got a whole pound of butter—more than we got back home. We tried to keep fit, with cricket, football, volleyball—first time I'd ever played that. We had a library, amateur theatricals, a camp orchestra. And we got news—someone always had a radio, somewhere. There were two parades a day, for head counts. We had a bad reputation in the RAF compound—mon-

keying around, insubordination. The guards would get mad with us. When you saw an Unteroffizier with steam coming off the top of his head and his hand fiddling at his holster, that was the time to back off. We were supposed to parade in rows of five, but there were always six or four in ours. That didn't do us much good, either. While the paratroops were back in their huts in the warm, we were still out there in the snow, being counted.

"There were some escape attempts. People under the rank of sergeant went out on working parties—sugar beet and stuff like that—and there was a possibility of swapping identities with one of them, but they were always caught and brought back. The Germans were up to all those tricks. We just had to stick it until the war ended. The Russians liberated us on April 23, 1945. I was flown home eventually via Brussels—the only time I was ever in a Lanc."

On March 4, 1945, RAF Bomber Command flew no major missions, and Joe Williams's

crew, based at Kelstern in Lincolnshire, had a whip-round (officers a pound, NCOs ten shillings) for an evening at the village pub. In the course of the party, through an alcoholic haze, rear gunner Williams heard something said about a spare parachute that was always stowed behind the pilot's seat. The words stayed in his mind.

Next night, over a thousand Lancasters and Halifaxes set off to continue *Operation Thunderclap*–a series of USAAF/RAF attacks on east German cities, requested by the Russians at the Yalta conference–which had opened with the Dresden holocaust on February 13. The main target for the heavies on March 5 was Chemnitz, near the Czech border, while a smaller force attacked the oil refinery at Böhlen.

The mission started badly: nine Halifaxes, flying from ice-bound Yorkshire bases, crashed on takeoff or immediately afterward. Williams's aircraft, flying in the third wave of the main attack, lost the starboard outer engine on the climb. Without the hydraulic pump driven by that engine,

the mid-upper gunner could neither fire his guns nor turn his turret. Worse still, Fox 2 could not reach the scheduled altitude of 18,000 feet and lagged behind the stream, losing all the protection of the "window" screen. The pilot, Canadian Jim Alexander, decided to continue, and Williams believed two factors influenced him: "A few nights earlier, a crew had aborted. Later in the mess, there were thinly veiled hints of cowardice. Also, back in September, Jim's elder brother had died piloting a Dakota over Arnhem. Jim was quietly determined to do the job."

There was little flak over Chemnitz, and the city was glowing in the light of many fires. As the bombload fell and Fox 2 turned away, Williams identified an enemy night fighter. He called, "Corkscrew starboard," and opened fire. The fighter, armed with upward-firing *Schräge Musik* guns, moved in below the bomber's tail.

"The cannon shells came banging in," said Williams, "all along the fuselage. Both wings were ablaze and the tail plane was fall-

Gestapo and people like that. They moved Dougie on after a bit, and in the end he escaped and came back, because it was near the Allied lines. He found his crew had put the fire out and got home safely. They all got bravery awards, but Dougie got a court-martial for desertion in the face of the enemy. Poor old Dougie."

Jack Clift, flight engineer, 463 Sqn.

left: In 1948 these B-17S near Munich are but skeletons. above: The remains of *Johnnie The Wolf*, a Halifax bomber that, amazingly, was able to make it back to base despite major engine damage on July 25, 1943, an almost certain abandonment that was somehow avoided.

right: The usual War
Department telegram,
below: The prisoner
identification card of
Roger A.Armstrong,
91BG, Bassingbourn

**War is as much a
punishment to the
punisher as to the
sufferer.**

—from *The Odyssey*, by
Homer

WESTERN UNION (00)

A. N. WILLIAMS
PRESIDENT

The filing time shown in the date line on telegrams and day letters is STANDARD TIME at point of origin. Time of receipt is STANDARD TIME at point of destination

MA201 35 GOVT=WASHINGTON DC 9 1109P

MRS NELLIE D ARMSTRONG=

615 WEST 19TH ST SIOUXFALLS SDAK=

1944 DEC 9 PM 11 01

REPORT JUST RECEIVED THROUGH THE INTERNATIONAL RED CROSS
STATES THAT YOUR SON SERGEANT ROGER W ARMSTRONG IS A
PRISONER OF WAR OF THE GERMAN GOVERNMENT LETTER OF
INFORMATION FOLLOWS FROM PROVOST MARSHAL GENERAL=

DUNLOP ACTING THE ADJUTANT GENERAL.

Figur:	kräftig	Augen:	grau
Größe:	1.74	Nase:	gerade
Schädelform:	längl.	Bart:	-
Haare:	braun	Gebiß:	gut
Gewicht:	65 kg		
Gesichtsform:	breit	Besondere Kennzeichen:	
Gesichtsfarbe:	gesund	Narbe an der linken Ferse	

Rechter Zeigefinger

Front   Profil   Fingerabdruck

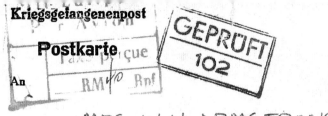

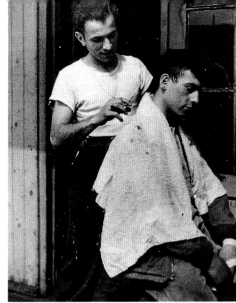

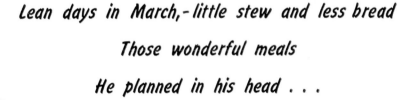

Lean days in March,- little stew and less bread

Those wonderful meals

He planned in his head . . .

above left: One of the postcards that Roger Armstrong mailed from Stalag Luft 1, center left: A page from a book of drawings by a USAAF POW, above and left: Images photographed at Stalag Luft 1.

17

ing off in lumps. Jim gave the order to bail out. I got the port-side turret door open. The turret was turned to the beam, and great sheets of flame were streaming past. I wound the turret straight with the manual gear, but I couldn't open the other door. I thought I was going to die. I shouted, 'For God's sake, get me out of here,' and when I tried the door again it opened. The flames were spiraling down the length of the fuselage and my parachute was burning in its stowage."

It was then that Williams remembered the "spare parachute." He fought his way to the cabin, but there was no chute behind the pilot's seat. He found it at last below the navigator's desk. Floating down through the darkness, his first thoughts were of his parents on the Sussex farm, and of their anguish when they received the inevitable telegram: "The Air Ministry regret to inform you . . ."

He landed on high heathland, buried his parachute and Mae West in the snow, and blew his aircrew whistle for a while. No one returned his signal. He considered his position: his burnt flesh needed treatment, he was deep in central Europe and very far from friends. He walked down the hillside and came to the back of an isolated farmhouse. A gleam of light showed from a small outbuilding set beside the path. He knocked and opened the door, which was promptly closed again. *"Engländer!"* he shouted, at which the occupant emerged and grabbed him by the shoulder. (Williams claims the distinction of being the only Allied airmen to give himself up to a German in a lavatory.)

"The family was roused," said Williams,

"and they were really kind. They gave me a drink of water, pointed to my burns, and suggested 'benzine,' to which I agreed. A daughter, who spoke some English, asked if I loved Mr. Churchill. I said we didn't 'love' politicians, and asked if they loved Hitler, at which there was a resounding *'Ja.'* The son was sent to fetch the Volksturm, and they arrived in slouch hats, carrying shotguns— just like our Home Guard. One of them patted his twelve-bore warningly (I was so glad to be alive that I laughed at him), and they took me to the local police house, where I spent the rest of the night. Next day, we walked to the nearest town, and I was taken to a doctor. In the crowded surgery, a woman insisted that I take her seat. The doctor treated my face, and I was put in a cell in another building. Late that night, the door was opened, someone said *'Kamerad,'* and my mid-upper gunner was pushed into the cell."

Williams and the gunner, now joined by three more members of his crew, were taken to Nuremberg in a crowded railway train. "Earlier in the day," Williams continued, "the city had been bombed, and a hostile crowd gathered round us. To their credit our young guards cocked their Tommy guns and the crowd left us alone. We boarded a train for Frankfurt. On the way, Allied fighters appeared overhead, the train stopped, the guards locked us in and scrambled up the embankment with everyone else. We took the opportunity to repossess all the edibles and the burns paste from our escape kit, which the guards had been carrying. The fighter planes did not attack and the journey to Frankfurt continued. After a few days in a cell I was taken to an interrogating officer. He said, 'Sit down, Williams, have a cigarette, how do you think the war is going?' A large folder headed '625 Squadron' was lying on his desk. 'When you took off from Kelstern,' he asked, 'how many aircraft were with you?' I said I'd never heard of Kelstern. 'Come, come,' he said, 'I know you are from Kelstern, and that you are in C flight.' He named the squadron and C flight commanders. 'And you must know Sergeant Hess, he was through here a few days ago. Unfortunately, he hurt his arm when he bailed out.' "

Williams was impressed, but he stuck to the rule of giving only name, rank, and number. The interrogation ended and he was taken to a transit camp, where he stayed, under treatment, while his crewmates were transported to Stalag Luft III near Nuremberg. On March 30, the camp was abandoned; the guards and POWs piled their kit into wagons and moved east. In a striking demonstration of Allied air superiority at that stage of the war, every form of transport in which the prisoners traveled was shot up. If it was not a pair of USAAF Thunderbolts splintering the wagons and frightening the horses, it was an RAF Mosquito derailing the trains. After that, the party moved on foot.

"In the evening," Williams recorded, "the column halted about eight miles south of Nuremberg and we were allowed to lie down under the trees in the corner of a wood beside the road. Bill asked if I still had my escape map. I said I had, and he said we ought to think about making a break for it. I said, 'How about now?' We turned on our stomachs and crawled past the guards into the wood."

For the next ten days, Williams and his crewmate lived the life of the evader, lying low by day and traveling by night. Always wet and hungry, always moving west, avoiding Allied bombs and German soldiers, they came upon the tracks of a Sherman tank. Next day, they found the U.S. Army, by whom they were welcomed, fed, medically examined, and, in due course, transported back to England.

below: In May 1945, *Operation Revival* was launched in which aircraft of various heavy bomber units were used to picl up Allied POWs and fly them back to points of Allied control. Here 91BG pilot Charles Sanzenbacher is being deloused after having flown a group of POWs from Barth, Germany, to Reims.

Sleep is the best cure for waking troubles.

—Cervantes

195

PATCHES

The bright, decorative squadron patch added identity to the uniform of American airmen in WWII. Examples of the patches are shown here as well as eight different versions of the 8AF patch.

365BS
305BG

323BS
91BG

551BS
385BG

548BS
385BG

713BS
448BG

570BS
390BG

401BS
91BG

365BS
305BG

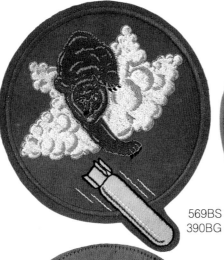

569BS
390BG

729BS
452BG

731BS
452BG

391BS
34BG

305BG

392BG

422BS
305BG

423BS
306BG

4BS
34BG

863BS
493BG

350BS
100BG

707BS
446BG

532BS
381BG

POTESTAS ACCURATIOQUE

379BG

44BG

TO THE BIG CITY

LAST NIGHT, some of the young gentlemen of the RAF took me to Berlin. The pilot was called Jock. The crew captains walked into the briefing room, looked at the maps and charts and sat down with their big celluloid pads on their knees. The atmosphere was that of a school and a church. The pilots were reminded that Berlin is Germany's greatest center of war production. The intelligence officer told us how many heavy and light ack-ack guns; how many searchlights we might expect to encounter. Then, Jock, the wing commander, explained the system of marking, the kind of flares that would be used by the pathfinders. He said that concentration was the secret of success in these raids; that as long as the aircraft stayed well bunched, they would protect each other. The captains of aircraft walked out. I noticed that the big Canadian with the slow, easy grin had printed Berlin at the top of his pad and then embellished it with a scroll. The red-headed English boy with the two-weeks'-old mustache was the last to leave the room.

Late in the afternoon we went to the locker room to draw parachutes, Mae Wests and all the rest. As we dressed a couple of Australians were whistling. Walking out to the bus that was to take us to the aircraft, I heard the station loudspeakers announcing that that evening all personnel would be able to see a film: *Star-Spangled Rhythm.* Free.

We went out and stood around the big, black four-motored Lancaster, D for Dog. A small station wagon delivered a thermos bottle of coffee, chewing gum, an orange and a bit of chocolate for each man. Up in that part of England the air hums and throbs with the sound of aircraft motors all day, but for half an hour before takeoff, the skies are dead, silent and expectant. A lone hawk hovered over the airfield, absolutely still as he faced into the wind. Jack, the tail gunner, said, "It'd be nice to fly like that." D-Dog eased around the perimeter track to the end of the runway. We sat there for a moment. The green light flashed and we were rolling . . . ten seconds ahead of schedule.

The takeoff was as smooth as silk. The wheels came up and D-Dog started the long climb. As we came up through the clouds I looked right and left and counted fourteen black Lancasters climbing for the place where men must burn oxygen to live. The sun was going down and its red glow made rivers and lakes of fire on the top of the clouds. Down to the southward, the clouds piled up to form castles, battlements and whole cities, all tinged with red.

Soon we were out over the North Sea. Dave, the navigator, asked Jock if he couldn't make a little more speed. We were nearly two minutes late. By this time, we were all using oxygen. The talk on the intercom was brief and crisp. Everyone sounded relaxed. For a while, the eight of us, in our little world of exile, moved over the sea. There was a quarter moon on the starboard beam and Jock's quiet voice came through the intercom, "That'll be flak ahead." We were approaching the enemy coast. The flak looked like a cigarette lighter in a dark room: one that won't light—sparks but no

Lie in the dark and listen/It's clear tonight so they're flying high/Hundreds of them, thousands perhaps Riding the icy, moonlit sky/ Men, machinery, bombs and maps Altimeters and guns and charts/ Coffee, sandwiches, fleece-lined boots/ Bones and muscles and minds and hearts English saplings with English roots/ Deep in the earth they've left below/ Lie in the dark and let them go/ Lie in the dark and listen.

—"Lie in the Dark and Listen," by Noël Coward

We judge ourselves by what we feel capable of doing,/ while others judge us by what we have already done.

—from "Kavanagh," by Henry Wadsworth Longfellow

EDWARD R.MURROW'S "THIS IS LONDON" BROADCAST OF DECEMBER 4, 1943

below: An RAF Stirling crew stands by as trolleys of bombs are brought up to be loaded for a raid on January 29, 1942.

flame—the sparks crackling just below the level of the cloud tops. We flew steady and straight and soon the flak was directly below us. D-Dog rocked a little from right to left but that wasn't caused by the flak. We were in the slipstream of other Lancasters ahead and we were over the enemy coast. Then a strange thing happened. The aircraft seemed to grow smaller. Jack in the rear turret, Wally the mid-upper gunner, Titch the wireless operator, all seemed somehow to draw closer to Jock in the cockpit. It was as though each man's shoulder was against the others. The understanding was complete. The intercom came to life and Jock said, "Two aircraft on the port beam." Jack in the tail said, "Okay, sir. They're Lancs." The whole crew was a unit and wasn't wasting words. The cloud below was ten-tenths. The blue-green jet of the exhausts licked back along the wing and there were other aircraft all around us. The whole great aerial armada was hurtling toward Berlin. We flew so for twenty minutes, when Jock looked up at a vapor trail curling above us, remarking in a conversational tone that, from the look of it, he thought there was a fighter on up there. Occasionally the angry red of the ack-ack burst through the clouds, but it was far away and we took only an academic interest. We were flying in the third wave.

Jock asked Wally in the mid-upper turret, and Jack in the rear, if they were cold. They said they were all right and thanked him for asking. He even asked how I was and I said, "All right so far." The cloud was beginning to thin out. Off to the north we could see lights and the flak began to liven up ahead of us. Buzz, the bomb-aimer, crackled through on the intercom, "There's a battle going on over on the starboard beam." We couldn't see the aircraft but we could see the jets of red tracer being exchanged. Suddenly, there was a burst of yellow flame and Jock remarked, "That's the fighter going down. Note the position." The whole thing was interesting, but remote. Dave, the navigator, who was sitting back with his maps, charts and compasses, said, "The attack ought to begin in exactly two minutes." We were still over the clouds.

But suddenly those dirty gray clouds turned white and we were over the outer searchlight defenses. The clouds below us were white and we were black. D-Dog seemed like a black bug on a white sheet. The flak began coming up, but none of it close. We were still a long way from Berlin. I didn't realize just how far. Jock observed, "There's a kite on fire dead ahead." It was a great, golden, slow-moving meteor slanting toward the earth. By this time we were about thirty miles from our target area in Berlin. That thirty miles was the longest flight I have ever made.

Dead on time, Buzz the bomb-aimer reported, "Target indicators going down." At the same moment, the sky ahead was lit up by bright yellow flares. Off to starboard another kite went down in flames. The flares were sprouting all over the sky, reds and greens and yellows, and we were flying straight for the center of the fireworks. D-Dog seemed to be standing still, the four

We had many famous and interesting visitors to the station during those years. In November 1943, Dame Laura Knight came for a lengthy stay, appointed official war artist to paint an RAF picture (hung at the Royal Academy the following year and now in the Imperial War Museum). I was made her guide in her search for a subject—a very happy association. She wasn't the least interested in inanimate subjects, obviously. She wanted life and drama, so one evening I did a very "not done" thing, and took her into an aircraft being prepared for take-off. The startled crew quickly responded to her excited outburst—"Oh, here's my picture—don't show me anything else!" So from then on she settled down to her picture entitled "Take-Off," with different crews only too willing to sit for her during their precious free time. She won all hearts during her stay with us and painted some beautiful crests on several of the aircraft. I very much treasure a small, signed, pen and ink copy she did for me of the wireless operator in her picture.

—from *We, Also Were There*, by "Archie" Hall, WAAF

left: "Take Off" by Dame Laura Knight.

propellers thrashing the air, but we didn't seem to be closing in. The cloud had cleared and off to the starboard a Lanc was caught by at least fourteen searchlight beams. We could see him twist and turn and finally break out. But still, the whole thing had a quality of unreality about it. No one seemed to be shooting at us, but it was getting lighter all the time. Suddenly, a tremendous big blob of yellow light appeared dead ahead; another to the right and another to the left. We were flying straight for them. Jock pointed out to me the dummy fires and flares to right and left, but we kept going in. Dead ahead there was a whole chain of red flares looking like stoplights. Another Lanc was coned on our starboard beam. The lights seemed to be supporting it. Again we could see those little bubbles of colored lead driving at it from two sides. The German fighters were at him. And then, with no warning at all, D-Dog was filled with an unhealthy white light.

I was standing just behind Jock and could see all the seams on the wings. His quiet Scots voice beat in my ears, "Steady lads, we've been coned." His slender body lifted half out of the seat as he jammed the control column forward and to the left. We were going down. Jock was wearing woolen gloves with the fingers cut off. I could see his fingernails turn white as he gripped the wheel. And then I was on my knees, flat on the deck, for he had whipped the Dog back into a climbing turn. The knees should have been strong enough to support me, but they weren't, and the stomach seemed in some

danger of letting me down too. I picked myself up and looked out again. It seemed that one big searchlight, instead of being twenty thousand feet below, was mounted right on our wing tip. D-Dog was corkscrewing. As we rolled down on the other side I began to see what was happening to Berlin.

The clouds were gone and the sticks of incendiaries from the preceding waves made the place look like a badly laid-out city with the streetlights on. The small incendiaries were going down like a fistful of white rice thrown on a piece of black velvet. As Jock hauled the Dog up again, I was thrown to the other side of the cockpit. And there below were more incendiaries, glowing white and then turning red. The cookies, the four-thousand-pound high explosive (bombs), were bursting below like great sunflowers gone mad. And then, as we started down again, still held in the lights, I remembered that the Dog still had one of those cookies and a whole basket of incendiaries in his belly, and the lights still held us, and I was very frightened.

While Jock was flinging us about in the air, he suddenly yelled over the intercom, "Two aircraft on the port beam." I looked astern and saw Wally, the mid-upper, whip his turret around to port, and then looked up to see a single-engine fighter slide just above us. The other aircraft was one of ours. Finally, we were out of the cone, flying level. I looked down and the white fires had turned red. They were beginning to merge and spread, just like butter does on a hot plate. Jock and Buzz, the bomb-aimer, began to discuss the target. The smoke was getting thick down below. Buzz said he liked the two green flares on the ground almost dead ahead. He began calling his directions. Just then a new bunch of big flares went down on the far side of the sea of flame that seemed to be directly below us. He thought that would be a better aiming point. Jock agreed and they flew on.

The bomb doors were opened. Buzz called his directions: "Five left, five left." And then, there was a gentle, confident upward thrust under my feet and Buzz said, "Cookie gone." A few seconds later, the incendiaries went, and D-Dog seemed lighter and easier to handle. I thought I could make out the outline of streets below, but the bomb-aimer didn't agree, and he ought to know. By this time, all those patches of white on black had turned yellow and started to flow together. Another searchlight caught us but didn't hold us. Then, through the intercom came the word, "One can of incendiaries didn't clear. We're still carrying it." And Jock replied, "Is it a big one or a little one?" The word came back: "Little one I think." Finally, the intercom announced that it was only a small container of incendiaries left, and Jock remarked, "Well, it's hardly worth going back and doing a run up for that." If there had been a good fat bundle left, he would have gone back through that stuff and done it all over again. I began to breathe, and to reflect again that all men would be brave if only they could leave their stomachs at home, when there was a tremendous *whoomph*, an unintelligible shout from the tail gunner, and D-Dog shivered and lost altitude. I looked to the port side and there was a Lancaster that seemed close enough to touch. He had whipped straight under us; missed us by twenty-five, fifty feet, no one knew how much.

The navigator sang out the new course and we were heading for home. Jock was doing what I had heard him tell his pilots to do so often—flying dead on course. He flew straight into a huge green searchlight, and as he rammed the throttles home he remarked, "We'll have a little trouble getting away from this one." Again D-Dog dove, climbed and twisted, and was finally free. We flew level then. I looked on the port beam at the target area. There was a red, sullen, obscene glare. The fires seemed to have found each other . . . and we were heading home.

For a little while it was smooth sailing. We saw more battles. Then another plane in flames, but no one could tell whether it was ours or theirs. We were still near the target. Dave said, "Hold her steady, skipper. I want to get an astral sight." Jock held her steady. And the flak began coming up at us. It seemed to be very close. It was winking off both wings, but the Dog was steady. Finally, Dave said, "Okay, skipper. Thank you very much." A great orange blob of flak smacked up straight in front of us, and Jock said. "I think they're shooting at us." I'd thought so for some time. He began to throw D for Dog up, around and about again. When we were clear of the barrage, I asked him how close the bursts were and he said, "Not very close. When they're really near, you can smell

As they watched it the bomber seemed to swell up very gently with a soft whoomp that was audible far across the sky. It became a ball of burning petrol, oil and pyrotechnic compounds. The yellow datum marker, which should have marked the approach to Krefeld, burned brightly as it fell away, leaving thin trails of sparks. The fireball changed from red to light pink as its rising temperature enabled it to devour new substances from hydraulic fluid and human fat to engine components of manganese, vanadium, and copper. Finally even the airframe burned. Ten tons of magnesium alloy flared with a strange greenish-blue light. It lit up the countryside beneath it like a slow flash of lightning and was gone. For a moment a cloud of dust illuminated by the searchlights floated in the sky and then even that disappeared.

—from *Bomber*, by Len Deighton

My candle burns at both ends;/ It will not last the night;/ But, ah, my foes, and, oh, my friends—It gives a lovely light.

—from *A Few Figs from Thistles*, by Edna St. Vincent Millay

below: The Lancaster Able "Mabel" is safely back from her 120th operation against German targets. Very few allied bomber aircraft achieved 100 or more missions in WWII.

'em." That proved nothing for I'd been holding my breath.

Jack sang out from the rear turret that his oxygen was getting low; he thought maybe the lead had frozen. Titch went scrambling back with a new mask and a bottle of oxygen. Dave said, "We're crossing the coast." My mind went back to the time I had crossed that coast in 1938, in a plane that had taken off from Prague. Just ahead of me sat two refugees from Vienna—an old man and his wife. The copilot came back and told them that we were outside German territory. The old man reached out and grabbed his wife's hand.

The work that was done last night was a massive blow of retribution, for all those who have fled from the sound of shots and blows on a stricken continent.

We began to lose height over the North Sea. We were over England's shores. The land was dark beneath us. Somewhere down there below, American boys were probably bombing up Fortresses and Liberators, getting ready for the day's work. We were over the home field. We called the control tower and the calm, clear voice of an English girl replied, "Greetings D-Dog. You are diverted to Mulebag." We swung round, contacted Mulebag, came in on a flare path, touched down very gently, ran along to the end of the runway and turned left. And Jock, the finest pilot in Bomber Command, said to the control tower, "D-Dog clear of runway."

When we went in for interrogation, I looked on the board and saw that the big, slow, smiling Canadian, and the red-headed English boy with the two-weeks'-old moustache hadn't made it. They were missing.

There were four reporters on this operation. Two of them didn't come back. Two friends of mine, Norman Stockton of Australian Associated Newspapers, and Lowell Bennett, an American representing International News Service. There is something of a tradition amongst reporters, that those who are prevented by circumstances from filing their stories, will be covered by their colleagues. This has been my effort to do so. In the aircraft in which I flew, the men who flew and fought poured into my ears their comments on fighters, flak and flares in the same tone that they would have used in reporting a host of daffodils. I have no doubt that Bennett and Stockton would have given you a better report of last night's activity.

Berlin was a thing of orchestrated Hell— a terrible symphony of light and flames.

[*Author's note:* Happily, Lowell Bennett made a safe return from the raid described in this broadcast.]

We managed to collect fairly complete information concerning the numbers of crewmen from missing aircraft of various types who turned up as prisoners of war. The numbers were startling. From the American bombers shot down in daylight, about 50 per cent escaped. From the older types of British night bomber, the Halifax and Stirling, about 25 per cent. From Lancasters, 15 per cent. It was easy to argue that the difference in the escape rate between the American bombers and the Halifaxes and Stirlings was attributable to the difference in circumstances between day and night bombing. The Americans may have had more warning before they were hit and more time to organize their departure. It was obviously easier to find the way out by daylight than in the dark. No such excuses could account for the difference between the Halifaxes and the Lancasters. The explanation was that the Lancaster hatch was in various ways more awkward, and harder to squeeze through. The awkwardness probably cost the lives of several thousand boys."

Article in *The Observer* magazine, October 28, 1977, by Freeman Dyson, wartime member of the Operational Research Section, RAF Bomber Command HQ.

ROUND THE CLOCK

BETWEEN AUGUST 17, 1942, and April 25, 1945, the U.S. Eighth Air Force dropped almost 700,000 tons of bombs on European targets, and it was fitting that the last should fall from a B-17 based at Grafton Underwood, the field that had launched Ira Eaker's gallant force on the first American bomber mission of the war. The wheel had turned full circle: those dozen early Fortresses had become the "Mighty Eighth"—the most powerful air bombardment force the world had ever seen. With the aid of the Ninth Air Force, based in England since October 1943, and of the Fifteenth operating from the south, the Eighth and the British had conquered the Luftwaffe, destroyed Hitler's oil industry, smashed his roads and railways, immobilized his battleships, ruined his dockyards and U-boat pens, and nullified his V-weapons; in German towns and cities, over a million able-bodied men had been employed in manning the defenses, trying to fight the fires and clear away the debris. Together, the bomber fleets had paved the way for *Overlord* and Eisenhower's advance.

By late April 1945, the 1st U.S. Army had fought its way through Halle and Leipzig street by street; to the north, the Magdeburg garrison had needed the attentions of a medium bomber group and a full Corps assault by the 9th U.S. Army to bring it down. Further north, the British 2nd Army had reached the river Weser south of Bremen and the Elbe south of Hamburg. Approaching from the east, Red Army tank commanders could train their binoculars on the buildings—such as were still standing—in the suburbs of Berlin.

"We were running out of targets," said Lawrence Drew of the 384th Bomb Group. "We didn't know where the Russians were going to be, and we didn't always know where General Patton was going to be." The Eighth was undertaking "quickies"—missions laid on at short notice to meet a tactical requirement. "We would think we had the day off," Drew recalled, "and then the sirens would blast and there would be a call for everyone to run to the flight line and get off the ground as quickly as we could, on account of some bit of intelligence the Air Force had received. Some of those quickies were just as rough as the regular missions."

On April 25, while American soldiers, moving east, were making the first contact with their Russian allies at the town of Torgau on the river Elbe, some two hundred B-17s of the 1st Air Division attacked the Skoda armament factory in Pilsen, Czechoslovakia, another force bombed the nearby airfield, and the 2nd Air Division's B-24s struck at railway terminals in southeastern Germany. For the factory attack, the lead crews had been ordered to bomb visually or not at all; despite the risk of alerting the defenses, messages had been broadcast on Radio Free Europe warning the Czech workers to stay out of the plant.

Piloting the lead aircraft of Grafton Underwood's high squadron was a Captain McCartney, the operations officer; Captain Fisher was the lead bombardier, Lieutenant Schultz the navigator, and Technical Sergeant Lustig the radio operator. After bomb

Many strokes, though with a little axe, hew down and fell the hardest-timber'd oak.

—from *Henry VI*, Part III, Act II, Sc. I, by William Shakespeare

"Some of our most interesting radio programs come from Germany. Lord Haw-Haw keeps us amused twice an evening."

Keith Newhouse, pilot, 467BG

below: William Joyce, a British fascist, who broadcast propaganda from Hamburg for the Nazis, was known to the Allies as Lord Haw Haw, above right: The interrogation of a RAF Stirling crew after the raid of August 23-24, 1943, on Berlin.

release, it would be David Lustig's task to trigger the camera for the photo of the impact point, check the bomb bay for hang-ups, and transmit a coded report of the results.

On the bomb run, drifting cloud obscured the aiming point: Fisher stopped his countdown and told McCartney to abort the run. McCartney swung away; maintaining their stations, Lawrence Drew and the other squadron pilots followed him. Slowly, the twelve-plane formation circuited the target and made a new approach. By then, the flak had found their altitude and their course. "They're tracking us, Mac," the navigator called, "take evasive action."

"Fisher has the plane now, Schultz," drawled McCartney.

The bombardier began another countdown to release. "Five, four, three, two—take it around, Mac." Again the entire formation wheeled and returned to the initial point. The 547th Squadron had led the group into the target: now they had the sky over Pilsen to themselves.

It was third time lucky for Lieutenant Fisher. His twelve 250-pounders fell toward the factory, and he called, "Bombs away." Instantly, the squadron toggleers released their loads. Down went Lawrence Drew's bombs and, from *Swamp Angel*, bringing up the rear, went the last to fall. In the lead plane, Lustig took the photograph, opened the door into the bomb bay, and pronounced it clear. A few seconds later, Fisher spoke again: "Bombardier to radio—bombed the primary target, results very good." Lustig

tapped out the last bomb-strike message of the Eighth Air Force's war.

It had been Drew's thirty-first mission with the 547th Squadron. "It was a pretty long trip, some twelve or thirteen hours, which kind of pushed the range of the B-17. Every time we went around the target, the flak got a little more accurate. We got so shot up—two engines out and any number of holes in the airplane—that I had to land at Lille, a base in France. My engineer and some of the crew found a wrecked B-24, and stripped some parts off it to patch us up. We got back to Grafton Underwood about midnight. It was quite a note to finish on."

Six Fortresses were missing from the missions of the day, and thirty times that number suffered damage from the flak. Four hundred P-51s flew escort for the bombers, but so dire were the straits to which the once all-conquering Luftwaffe had been brought that the Mustang pilots found no more than a lone jet fighter to claim as their last kill.

The scrupulous efforts made on that last mission to minimize noncombatant casualties, at whatever hazard to the bomber crews, exemplified the methods of the USAAF in the European war. Although the policy had slipped a little now and then (eight Berlin attacks within the last twelve months had been on "the city area"), precision bombing had been the policy to start with, and despite all the problems occasioned by the weather, especially in winter, it had remained so to the end. Of course, there had been times when the airmen of the Eighth had been obliged to settle for the

"You couldn't let yourself think about bombing people. You knew they were down there, but you got to the point where you could just blank that out. Targets—that's what you had to think in terms of."

Frank Nelson, navigator, 487BG

The total number of British officers killed during the First World War, including the Royal Navy and the RAF, was 38,834. The total number of air crew of Bomber Command, exactly the same type of men, killed during the Second World War was 55,573.... During World War Two, RAF Bomber Command lost a total of 10,724 aircraft, of which 6,931 were heavy bombers including 2,232 Halifaxes and 3,832 Lancasters. The United States Eighth Air Force, which flew from the United Kingdom and formed the daylight component of the bombing offensive, also suffered cruelly, losing 4,754 B-17 Flying Fortresses and 2,112 B-24 Liberators out of total losses of 9,057 aircraft, most of the remainder being fighter escorts. 44,472 air crew of the United States Eighth Air Force lost their lives. More than 100,000 British, Commonwealth and American air crew of RAF Bomber Command and the United States Eighth Air Force were killed, all physically fit young men who were also able to comply with the exacting standards of air crew.

—from *Yesterday's Gone*, by N. J. Crisp

lesser option—radar target-marking—but, like the RAF, they had done the best they could with what they had. An American general, addressing the RAF Historical Society in 1991, summed up the matter with modesty and wit: "If you carried out area bombing, maybe what we did was precision area bombing."

While the attack on Pilsen was in progress, Eighth Air Force Mustangs were escorting 360 RAF Lancasters to the German Führer's stronghold at Berchtesgaden, high in the Bavarian Alps. The "Eagle's Nest," however, was shrouded in mist, and the *Oboe* radar beams on which the pathfinders depended were deflected by the mountains. Only fifty-three crews claimed to have hit the target. That same night a smaller force of Lancasters successfully attacked an oil refinery in southern Norway, and with that operation, the air campaign against Hitler's *Festung Europa* ended. In four and a half years, RAF aircrews had dropped 955,000 tons of high explosive and incendiaries. From that night on, neither they nor their partners in the mighty Eighth would carry bombs to Europe; *Thunderclap* and *Grayling* would never be repeated, *Crossbow* and *Gomorrah* were battles of the past. The tasks now were *Exodus*, bringing home their comrades from German prison camps, and *Operation Manna*, carrying provisions to the starving Dutch.

Like many others, Alan Forman believes that neither the RAF bomber crews nor their commander ever quite received the credit they were due. "The Americans were different; they appreciated what was done. They struck campaign medals. But we never struck a medal for Bomber Command—just a clasp on the Aircrew Europe Star. Harris was very upset about that. And he was given no recognition until later in his life. He went off to South Africa more or less with his tail between his legs. He was criticized for a lot of the big raids like Nuremberg and Dresden. I'm sure they weren't done on his decision—that would be political."

It is true that Arthur Harris left the scene comparatively unhonored and unsung, not an unknown fate for a British war leader. He was a dedicated, resolute commander, and for those of his superiors who did not share his commitment to the heavy bomber he had little time and less respect. For his American partners he had both. "If I were asked," he later wrote, "what were the relations between Bomber Command and the American bomber force I should say that we had no relations. The word is inapplicable to what actually happened; we and they were one force. The Americans gave us the best they had, and they gave us everything we needed as and when the need arose. I hope, indeed I know, that we did everything possible for them in turn. We could have no better brothers in arms than Ira Eaker, Fred Anderson and Jimmy Doolittle, and the Americans could have had no better commanders than these three. As for the American bomber crews, they were the bravest of the brave, and I know that I am speaking for my own bomber crews when I pay this tribute."

385BG airmen relaxing in Cambridge. L. to r: Mike Kyndia, Walter Oates, Bob Silver, "Lieb" Lieberthal, and George "Buzz" Sawyer.

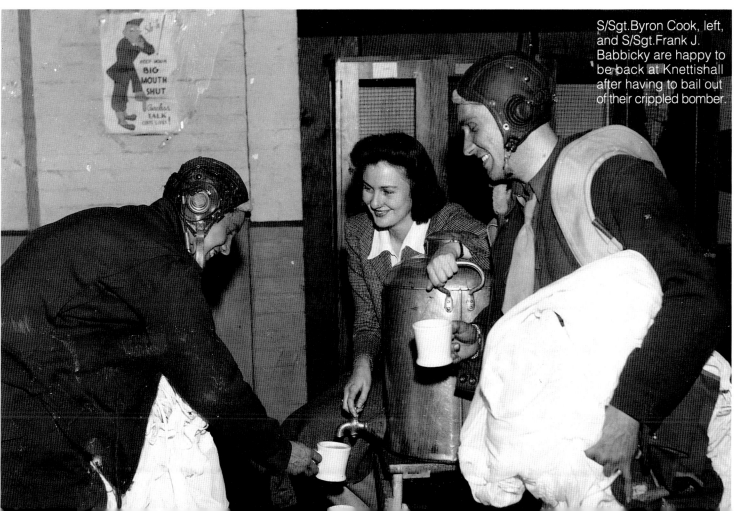

S/Sgt.Byron Cook, left, and S/Sgt.Frank J. Babbicky are happy to be back at Knettishall after having to bail out of their crippled bomber.

Peace and rest at length
have come,/ All the
day's long toil is past;
And each heart is
whispering "Home,
Home at last!"

—from "Home At Last,"
by Thomas Hood

above: The 385BG drops
food supplies to
the people of Rotterdam
on May 2, 1945, right:
93BG airmen at ease in
their Hardwick Nissen.

212

Few of the many thousands of young airmen who set out on bomber missions took a pessimistic view of their chances of survival: they had, were required to have, confidence in each other, in their aircraft and themselves. Of course, they sometimes dreaded what they had to do, and sometimes wished they didn't have to go, but mostly they believed they would come back; and, indeed, from any given mission, the majority did survive to fly and fight again. Of their number, however, some were bound to die, some to suffer mutilation, and some to fall, either wounded or unscathed, into the hands of the enemy. All would live through hours of chill discomfort, through moments of ela-tion and of fear; all would remember until their dying day how it felt when the fighters wheeled toward them, and when the flak defenses seemed to make a solid wall. The final tally of over 100,000 dead from the two bomber forces was the price the Allies paid for their campaign of bombing round the clock. Those men's sacrifice, and the unremitting efforts of their surviving comrades, made D-Day possible without a dreadful death toll on the beaches and the battlefields, and ensured that VE-Day would come.

Larry Bird summed up his feelings by saying: "My war career was not that fabulous, and I don't know whether I'd want to do it over or not. I don't think I was cut out for that kind of work, and I was pretty scared most of the time. But faced with doing it or else, I did it."

And this I hate—not men, nor flag nor race, But only War with its wild, grinning face.

—from "The Hymn of Hate," by Joseph Dana Miller

Sorrows are like thunderclouds—in the distance they look black, over our heads scarcely gray.

—from *Hesperus*, by Jean Paul Richter

In groups of 24, these British ex-POWs are being flown from Lubeck, Germany, to England on May 11, 1945, by Lancaster crews of RAF Bomber Command.

WEEDS

"We went back to Nuthampstead in 1962, and had trouble finding it. We went into The Woodman Inn and asked where the field was. They said to walk down this path about half a mile and you'll see it. Sure enough, we walked down the path and you could just see a few of the Quonset huts left. That was all."

Bill Ganz, 398BG

"All that's left of Skellingthorpe is a short piece of the perimeter track, a few buildings in the woods, and the remains of the bomb dump. There's a huge housing estate where the airfield used to be, with fourteen thousand people living on it. The Lincoln City Council let us use the leisure center for our squadron reunions. We have a forties night and a service at the memorial."

Reg Payne, wireless operator, 50 Sqn.

Man is born unto trouble, as the sparks fly upward.

–Job 5:7.

. . . he walked through the winding old streets of Archbury direct to a pub called the Black Swan, borrowed a bicycle from the bartender, slung his package to the handlebars and pedaled out of the village along a country road lined with hedges and shaggy houses with thatched roofs. Presently he turned off on a side road, propped his bike against a hedge and strode slowly a hundred yards out onto an enormous flat, unobstructed field. When he halted he was standing at the head of a wide, dilapidated avenue of concrete, which stretched in front of him with gentle undulations for a mile and a half. A herd of cows, nibbling at the tall grass which had grown up through the cracks, helped to camouflage his recollection of the huge runway. He noted the black streaks left by tires, where they had struck the surface, smoking, and nearby, through the weeds which nearly covered it, he could still see the stains left by puddles of grease and black oil on one of the hard-stands evenly spaced around the five-mile circumference of the perimeter track, like teeth on a ring gear. And in the background he could make out a forlorn dark green control tower, surmounted by a tattered gray windsock and behind it two empty hangars, a shoe box of a water tank on high stilts and an ugly cluster of squat Nissen huts. Not a soul was visible, nothing moved save the cows, nor was there any sound to break the great quiet. A gust of wind blew back the tall weeds behind the hard-stand nearest him. But suddenly Stovall could no longer see the bent-back weeds through the quick tears that blurred his eyes and slid down the deep lines in his face. He made no move to brush them away. For behind the blur he could see, from within, more clearly. On each empty hard-stand there sat the ghost of a B-17, its four whirling propellers blasting the tall grass with the gale of its slip stream, its tires bulging under the weight of tons of bombs and tons of the gasoline needed for a deep penetration.

–from *Twelve O'Clock High*, by Beirne Lay, Jr., and Sy Bartlett

right: Movie legend Jimmy Stewart revisiting his old 445BG base at Tibenham. Stewart also served as Operations Officer of the 453BG at Old Buckenham.

214

far left: Still tempting after all these years... at Bungay (Flixton), center left: The cinema at Framlingham in1985, left: Communications Section at Deenethorpe, below left: The derelict control tower at the 401BG Deenethorpe base, below: A runway at Deenethorpe, still in good condition in 1992.

left: War wrought tragic accidents as well as losses due to combat. This is the result of a taxiing accident at Thorpe Abbotts on December 27, 1943, above: Looking down on some of the 4,200 heavy bombers in repose at Walnut Ridge, Arkansas in November of 1945. The planes were stripped, chopped and smelted to convert them into a light metal reserve.

LET LIGHT PERPETUAL SHINE UPON THEM

THIS WINDOW COMMEMORATES THE EIGHT HUNDRED AND ONE AIRMEN OF 405 SQUADRON ROYAL CANADIAN AIRFORCE WHO GAVE THEIR LIVES – 1941-1945

THE BOMBER COMMAND MEMORIAL

An age builds up cities: an hour destroys them.

—Seneca

above: A memorial window at Great Gransden, top center: The restored control tower at East Kirkby, center left: A mess hall entrance at Ridgewell, center right: Speed limit still showing on a Maycrete hut at Tholthorpe, right: The splendid memorial to the members of the 401BG at Deenethorpe, with the old control tower visible behind the memorial.

TO REMEMBER THE

401st BOMBARDMENT GROUP H

8th UNITED STATES ARMY AIR FORCE
STATION 128 - DEENETHORPE
OCTOBER 1943 - JUNE 1945

612th SQUADRON

613th SQUADRON

614th SQUADRON

615th SQUADRON

From This Airfield The Gallant Men Of The 401st Flew 254 Combat Missions Over Germany And Occupied Europe In Sturdy B-17 Aircraft. The Group Was Awarded Two Distinguished Unit Citations And Had The Best Bombing Accuracy Record And Second Lowest Loss Ratio Among B-17 Groups In The 8th Air Force.

THE BEST DAMNED OUTFIT IN THE USAAF

DEDICATED SEPTEMBER 1989
401st BOMBARDMENT GROUP

above left: RAF Bomber Command window in the Lincoln cathedral, above: A rare training dome structure at the former RAF Langham, above right: The huge Dambusters memorial to 617 Squadron, at Woodhall Spa, Lincs., commemorating their historic raid of May 16, 1943, on the Mohne, Eder, Sorpe and Schwelme dams, below: The disused tower at Little Snoring, a former RAF Mosquito base.

above: The 491BG control tower at North Pickenham, below: A wounded airman being helped from his bomber at Kimbolton, right: WAAF barrage balloon operators.

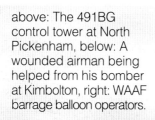

RV 5197

MEMORIAL
DEDICATED TO THE MEN OF THE
487TH BOMB GROUP (H)
WHO SACRIFICED THEIR LIVES IN WORLD WAR II, THAT THE IDEALS
OF DEMOCRACY MIGHT LIVE.

above: The Lavenham village square memorial to the 487BG, above right: An original hut marker from Lavenham, below: A reunion of 487BG veterans and their family members at Lavenham in the summer of 1992.

History is something that never happened, written by a man who wasn't there.

—Anonymous

ROYAL AIR FORCE
WICKENBY
No 1· GROUP BOMBER COMMAND
1942–1945

IN MEMORY OF
ONE THOUSAND AND EIGHTY MEN
OF 12 & 626 SQUADRONS
WHO GAVE THEIR LIVES ON
OPERATIONS FROM THIS AIRFIELD
IN THE OFFENSIVE AGAINST GERMANY
AND THE LIBERATION
OF OCCUPIED EUROPE
Per ardua ad astra

NOTICE
NO LOITERING
N OR AROUND
THIS POST

far left: The RAF Wickenby memorial, left: An original guard post sign from the Grafton Underwood base, below left: The Faith Winter statue of Marshal of the Royal Air Force Sir Arthur T. Harris, unveiled at St. Clement Danes church, London, in 1992. Harris, called 'Bomber' by the British press and 'Butch' (for Butcher) by aircrew, has been vilified for the area bombing of German cities in WWII, below: The Mendlesham memorial.

TO THE AMERICAN AIRMEN
OF THE '34TH', WHO, IN VALOR
GAVE THEIR LIVES TO THE VICTORY
THAT MADE REAL THE CHALLENGE
FOR WORLD PEACE AND UNITY

THE 34TH HEAVY BOMBARDMENT GROUP
A UNIT OF THE UNITED STATES
EIGHTH AIR FORCE
IN WORLD WAR II
APRIL 1944 TO JUNE 1945
MENDLESHAM AERO
DROME SUFFOLK

Heavy bombers of the
USAAF waiting to be
scrapped at Kingman,
Arizona in 1946.

I am not now that which
I have been.

—from *Childe Harold*, by
Lord Byron

below: Day's end on the old airfield at Lavenham, Suffolk, in summer 1992. right: A surviving shelter trench at RAF Woodhall Spa, below right: Anyone who wanted to could buy one or more WWII aircraft at the Cal-Aero sales storage depot of the Reconstruction Finance Corporation, Ontario, California in January 1946. Some of the planes were worn out, but many were bargains in excellent condition.

"I went back to my old base at Debach in 1976. A farmer owned the land. The field was all ploughed up, but the runways were still there. We got off the track and into that battle-bush or whatever it is that grows everywhere. It was doggone sharp . . ."

Larry Bird, toggleer, 493BG

Mr Roger Johnson, a former American airman who stole a cycle while stationed at Polebrook, Northants, during the Second World War, will make amends today by presenting 90 new ones costing nearly £10,000 to local children.

ROUND THE CLOCK

CONCEPT, DEVELOPMENT, EDITING,
PRIMARY RESEARCH, COLOR PHOTOGRAPHY,
AND BOOK DESIGN: PHILIP KAPLAN

TEXT: JACK CURRIE

PICTURE CREDITS

Photographs by Philip Kaplan are credited: PK. Photographs from the author's collection are credited: AC.

Jacket front: PK; jacket back: PK; jacket back flap--Philip Kaplan: Margaret Mayhew; jacket back flap--Jack Currie: PK. Title spread: PK. Front endsheet: USAF, back endsheet: AC.

DOING IT IN BROAD DAYLIGHT P2: Imperial War Museum, P3: Imperial War Museum, P4: AC, P5: AC, P6: AC, P7: USAF, P8: Imperial War Museum, P9 top and bottom: Imperial War Museum, P10: RAF Museum, P11: AC.

ALLIES P12-13 Charles Cundall painting/Imperial War Museum, P14: Imperial War Museum, P15: Quentin Bland, P16 top and bottom: PK, top center: Mark Brown-USAF Academy, P17: top and right: PK, center: Mark Brown-USAF Academy, P18: USAF, P19: Toni Frissell-Library of Congress, P20 both: PK, P21 all: PK, P22: AC.

GETTING UP FOR A MISSION P24-25: Mark Brown-USAF Academy, P26 top left: Quentin Bland, top right: USAF, bottom: USAF, P27 top: AC, bottom: John Archer, P28: Toni Frissell-Library of Congress, P29 both: Mark Brown-USAF Academy, P30 top left and bottom: Imperial War Museum, top right: AC, P31: AC, P32 all: PK, P33 all: PK.

KEY TARGETS P34: Popperfoto, P36 top left and right: Toni Frissell-Library of Congress, bottom: Mark Brown-USAF Academy, P37: PK, P39: USAF Academy, P40: PK, P41 left: AC, right: Toni Frissell-Library of Congress, bottom: Danesfield House.

TAKEOFF AND ASSEMBLY P42-43: USAF, P44 top left: USAF, center and bottom: PK, P45: Mark Brown-USAF Academy, P46: Toni Frissell-Library of Congress, P48 both: PK, P49 both: PK, P50: Imperial War Museum, P51 top: John Archer, bottom left: Major General Dale O.Smith, USAF (Ret), bottom right: Toni Frissell-Library of Congress, P53: Dennis Wrynn.

BASE ROUTINE P55: USAF Academy, P56 left: PK, right: Imperial War Museum, P57 all: PK, P58: USAF, P59 both: John Archer, P60 left and both center: PK, top right: Popperfoto, bottom: USAF Academy, P61: USAF Academy, P62 left: Ian Hawkins, top and bottom: Toni Frissell-Library of Congress, P63 top: USAF, bottom: Edith Kup, P65 top left: USAF, top right: USAF Academy, bottom: PK.

WAR IN THE AIR P66: Toni Frissell-Library of Congress, P68: A Frank Wootton painting: Frank Wootton, P69 top: USAF, center: PK, P71 top: Merle Olmsted Collection, bottom: Popperfoto, P72: Roger A.Armstrong, P73: courtesy Empire Press, P74: USAF Museum, P75: AC, P76 both: PK, P77 left: PK, right: USAF Museum.

HOME SWEET HOME P78: Jim Dacey, P80 all: PK, P81: PK, P82 top: John Archer, center right: John Archer, bottom right: John Archer, bottom left: USAF Academy, P83 top: John Archer, bottom: Ron Bicker, P84: Roland Hammersley, P85: AC, P86 top: USAF Academy, bottom: John Pawsey, P87: USAF, P88 top: PK, bottom left: Neal Kaplan, bottom right: Mark Brown-USAF Academy, P89 top and bottom left: PK, right: Roland Hammersley, P90: USAF Museum, P91 both: John Archer, P92 both: PK, P93 all: PK.

ON THE NOSE P94: Mark Brown-USAF Museum, P95 top left: USAF Academy, bottom left: John Archer, top right: John Archer, center and bottom right: USAF Academy, P96: Popperfoto, P97 top left: PK, all others: USAF Academy, P98 center right: Merle Olmsted Collection, all others: USAF Academy, P99 top left and center: John Archer, top right and bottom: USAF Academy, P100 all: USAF Academy, P101 top left and bottom: USAF Academy, top right: Mark Brown-USAF Academy, P102: USAF Academy, P103 top: USAF Academy, bottom: AC, P104: Popperfoto, P105 both: Mark Brown-USAF Academy.

AN AMERICAN RAID P106: Roger A. Armstrong, P107: USAF Academy, P108: PK, P109: Merle Olmsted Collection, P110: AC, P111: USAF, P112 top: USAF Academy, bottom: AC, P113 top: Toni Frissell-Library of Congress, bottom: John Archer, P114: Toni Frissell-Library of Congress, P115: Toni Frissell-Library of Congress, P116: AC, P117 top: Roger A.Armstrong, bottom: PK, P118: USAF, P119 all: USAF Academy.

DINGHY, DINGHY, PREPARE TO DITCH! P120-121: AC, P124 both: AC.

COUNTRY FOLK P127: Quentin Bland, P128: Jim Dacey, P129 John Askins, P130 top: John Pawsey, bottom: John Archer, P132 top left: PK, top and bottom right: PK, bottom left: Joe DeShay Collection via Merle Olmsted.

THE HARDWARE P134: Popperfoto, P136 top left and bottom: AC, top right: Mark Brown-USAF Academy, P137: AC, P138: AC, P139 top and bottom left: AC, bottom right: Popperfoto, P140 top: Mark Brown-USAF Academy, P141 top: USAF, bottom: Mark Brown-USAF Academy, P142: USAF Museum, P143: courtesy of *Crosshairs* magazine, P144 all: PK, P145: PK, P146 both: AC, P147: AC.

MUD AND MUSCLE P148: Popperfoto, P149: PK, P151: USAF.

AIRCREW P153: Imperial War Museum, P154: USAF Academy, P155 top left and right: USAF Academy, bottom: USAF Museum, P156: Imperial War Museum, P157 top left: Jack Woods, bottom left: PK, right: Nick Kosciuk, P158: courtesy Empire Press, P159 top and bottom: Imperial War Museum, P160 top left: Toni Frissell-Library of Congress, top right: Lloyd Stovall, bottom left: Jim Dacey, bottom center and right: USAF Academy, P162: The 100BG

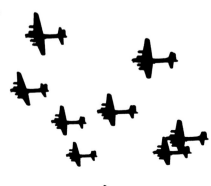

Memorial Museum, P163 top: PK, bottom: USAF Academy.

JACKETS P164 all: Dave Hill, P165 top and center: Dave Hill, top and center right and bottom two: Greg Parlin.

A BRITISH RAID P166: S/L Jack Currie, P168 top left and right: PK, bottom: AC, P169: PK, P170: AC, P171: AC, P172 all: PK, P173 both: PK, P175: Imperial War Museum, P177 A Frank Wootton painting: Frank Wootton, P178 top left and right: AC, bottom: BFI Stills, Posters & Designs, P180: USAF Academy, P181: PK, P182 top: AC, bottom: Imperial War Museum.

ABANDON! P184: courtesy Empire Press, P185: AC, P187: Albert Tyler, P188 both: PK via Albert Tyler, P189: PK, P190: Merle Olmsted Collection, P191: Imperial War Museum, P192 both: Roger A. Armstrong, P193 all: Roger A. Armstrong, P195: George Jacobs via Roger Armstrong.

PATCHES P196 all: Greg Parlin, P197 all: Dave Hill.

TO THE BIG CITY P199: Popperfoto, P200: Imperial War Museum, P204: AC.

ROUND THE CLOCK P207: Toni Frisell-LibraryofCongress, P208: courtesy Empire Press, P209 both: AC, P211 top: Jim Dacey, bottom: USAF Academy, P212 top: Mark Brown-USAF Academy, bottom: John Archer, P213: Imperial War Museum.

WEEDS P215: Photographers International via John Archer Collection, P216 all: PK, P217 both: PK, P218: USAF Academy, P219: AC, P220 all: PK, P221 all: PK, P222 top: John Archer, bottom: Toni Frissell-Library of Congress, P223: Tangmere Military Aviation Museum, P224 all: PK, P225 all: PK, PP226-227: William T. Larkins via Michael O'Leary, P228: PK, P229 top: PK, bottom: AC, P233: PK.

ACKNOWLEDGMENTS

We are grateful to Margaret Kaplan and Kate Currie, our ever-thoughtful, patient, always supportive wives, for their help and good counsel, and all that they have done for *Round the Clock*.

We thank the following people, whose generous assistance has contributed greatly to the development of this book.

Fred Allen, John Archer, Roger A. Armstrong, Beth and David Alston, Eric Barnard, Malcolm Bates, Mike Benarcik, Robert Best, Ron Bicker, Larry Bird, Quentin Bland, Charles Bosshardt, Beverly Brannin, Sam Burchell, Leonard Cheshire, Paul Chryst, Jack Clift, Jim Dacey, E.W.Deacon, James H. Doolittle, Lawrence Drew, Ira Eakin, Gary Eastman, Gilly Fielder, W.W.Ford, Alan Forman, Carsten Fries, Bill Ganz, Stephen Grey, Roland Hammersley, Ian Hawkins, Air Vice Marshal P.M.S. Hedgeland, RAF, Dave Hill, Franc Isla, Claire Kaplan, Joseph Kaplan, Neal Kaplan, Paul Kemp, Percy Kindred, Nick Kosciuk, Edith Kup,William T.Larkins,

Robert D. Loomis, David C. Lustig, Donald Maffett, Ella Mayhew, Dickie Mayes, Cheryl Mathews, Mike Mathews, Tilly McMaster, Frank Nelson, Keith Newhouse, Michael O'Leary, Merle Olmsted, Greg Parlin, Tony Partridge, Colin Paterson, John Pawsey, L.W.Pilgrim, Reg Payne, Photographers International, Douglas Radcliffe, Sidney Rapoport, Lynn Ray, Duane J. Reed, Alan Reeves, Ted Richardson, Kay Riley, Charles Schindell, Dave Shelhamer, Paul Sink, Major General Dale O. Smith, Anne and Richard Stamp, Tony Starcer, James Stewart, Ken Stone, Lloyd Stovall, Calvin A. Swaffer, John B.Thomas, Jr., Leonard Thompson, Albert Tyler, William Vogt, David Wade, Tim Wells, Robert White, Ray Wild, Joe Williams, Jack Woods, Dennis Wrynn, Sam Young.

Grateful acknowledgment is made to the following for permission to reprint previously published material:

AIR FORCE magazine: Obituary of Forrest L.Vosler from the April 1992 issue of Air Force magazine. Copyright © 1992 by the Air Force Association. Reprinted by permission.

AIRLIFE PUBLISHING LIMITED: Excerpt from *Bomber Battle For Berlin* by John Searby, published in 1991 by Airlife Publishing Limited, 101 Longden Road, Shrewsbury. Reprinted by permission.

A.P. WATT LTD: Twenty lines from "Sausage and Mash," seventeen lines from "King of the Castle," forty-seven lines from "The Englishman," and twelve lines from "Two Drinking Songs" from *Laughing All and Other Poems* by A.P. Herbert. Seventy-seven lines from "Come to Britain" from *Plain Jane* by A.P. Herbert. Reprinted by permission of A.P. Watt Ltd on behalf of Crystal Hale and Jocelyn Herbert.

"ARCHIE" HALL: Excerpt from *We, Also, Were There* by "Archie" Hall, published by Merlin Books. Reprinted by permission.

WILLIAM HEINEMANN LIMITED: Excerpts from *Bomb Run* by Spencer Dunmore. Reprinted by permission of William Heinemann Limited.

DAVID HIGHAM ASSOCIATES: Excerpts from *Enemy Coast Ahead* by Guy Gibson, published by Michael Joseph. Reprinted by permission of David Higham Associates.

MICHAEL IMISON PLAYWRIGHTS LTD.: Excerpt from "Lie in the Dark and Listen" by Noël Coward. Reprinted by permission.

WILLIAM MORROW AND COMPANY, INC. AND ACTON & DYSTEL, INC.: Excerpts from *Combat Crew* by John Comer. Copyright © 1988 by John Comer. Rights throughout the British Commonwealth are controlled by Acton & Dystel, Inc. Reprinted by permission of William Morrow and Company, Inc. and Acton & Dystel, Inc.

"April through September are the best months they have for weather over there. Usually in the winter months they have much more drizzle and fog. There was cloud cover on a great number of mornings. There were a few rare mornings when it was truly clear. And when that happened, everybody that went down to the line was just so enthralled—what a wonderful day, it's just absolutely gorgeous!"

Frank Nelson, navigator, 487BG

"We took off and climbed through dense fog, and that required the goddamnedest precision. We were reversing our course and reversing again, so the danger of collision was always there, until we finally broke out of the cloud. It was a good feeling to be in the lead ship, because we were first off the ground and constantly climbing."

Sidney Rapoport, radar operator, 94BG

The sun shines even on the wicked.

—Seneca

And I am tempted, I confess,/ To self-congratulation When I reflect that I possess The virtues of my nation, And daily let my neighbours see/ How different their lives might be/ If they would but be ruled by me— With a fa, la, la, fa, la, la, la, la, la, la, With a fa, la, la, la, la, la, la!

The simple mind and manly air,/ Not Brains so much as Breeding, With joie de vivre and savoir faire,/ Are constantly succeeding; Not men of words, we live to do, Nor speak till we are spoken to, The answer "Cock-a-doodle-doo!"— With a fa, la, la, fa, la, la, la, la, la, la, With a fa, la, la, la, la, la, la!

Alas, for all our kindly pain,/ The world is sick and sore, Sir, And Frenchmen mulishly remain/ As foreign as before, Sir./ Thus ends the tale as it began; Conceive the difference, if you can,/ Had Adam been an Englishman— With a fa, la, la, fa, la, la, la, la, la, la, With a fa, la, la, la, la, la, la!

—"The Englishman," by A. P. Herbert

True bravery is shown by performing without witness what one might be capable of doing before all the world.

—La Rochefoucauld

PENGUIN BOOKS USA INC. AND MURRAY POLLINGER: Excerpts from *Yesterday's Gone* by N.J.Crisp. Copyright ©1983 by N.J.Crisp. Published in Great Britain by Macdonald & Co. Ltd. Rights throughout Canada and the British Commonwealth are controlled by Murray Pollinger. Reprinted by permission of Viking Penguin, a division of Penguin Books USA Inc. and Murray Pollinger.

BIBLIOGRAPHY

Armstrong, Roger A., *USA the Hard Way*, Quail House, 1991.

Bekker, Cajus, *The Luftwaffe War Diaries*, Doubleday, 1968.

Bennett, Air Vice Marshal D.C.T., *Pathfinder*, Goodall, 1958.

Bramson, Alan, *Master Airman--A Biography of Air Vice Marshal Donald Bennett*, 1985.

Caidin, Martin, *Black Thursday*, E.P.Dutton Co., 1960.

Campbell, James, *The Bombing of Nuremberg*, Doubleday, 1974.

Charlwood, Don, *Journeys into Night*, Hudson, 1991.

Cheshire, Leonard, *Bomber Pilot*, Goodall, 1988.

Coffey, Thomas, *Iron Eagle*, Crown, 1986.

Comer, John, *Combat Crew*, William Morrow, 1988.

Crisp, N.J., *Yesterday's Gone*, Penguin, 1983.

Cumming, Michael, *Pathfinder Cranswick*, William Kimber, 1962.

Deighton, Len, *Bomber*, Harper and Row, 1970.

Dunmore, Spencer, *Bomb Run*, Pan Books, 1971.

Fletcher, Eugene, *Fletcher's Gang*, University of Washington Press, 1988.

Fletcher, Eugene, *The Lucky Bastard Club*, University of Washington Press, 1992.

Freeman, Roger A., *The Mighty Eighth*, Macdonald, 1970.

Freeman, Roger A., *The Mighty Eighth War Diary*, Jane's, 1981.

Freeman, Roger A., *The Mighty Eighth War Manual*, Jane's, 1984.

Gibson, Guy, *Enemy Coast Ahead*, Goodall, 1986.

Harris, Sir Arthur, *Bomber Offensive*, Collins, 1947.

Hastings, Max, *Bomber Command*, Michael Joseph, 1979.

Hawkins, Ian, *The Munster Raid*, Aero/Tab Books, 1990.

Hersey, John, *The War Lover*, Alfred A.Knopf, 1959.

Hutton, Bud, and Andy Rooney, *Air Gunner*, Farrar & Rinehart, 1944.

Jablonski, Edward, *Flying Fortress*, Doubleday, 1965.

Kantor, Mackinlay, *Mission with LeMay*, Doubleday, 1965.

Koger, Fred, *Countdown*, Algonquin Books, 1990.

Lay, Jr., Beirne, and Sy Bartlett, *12 O'Clock High!*, Ballantine Books, 1948.

Longmate, Norman, *The Bombers*, Arrow Books, 1988.

Maurer, Maurer, *Air Force Combat Units of World War II*, Franklin Watts, Inc., 1963.

Michie, Allan A., *The Air Offensive Against Germany*, Henry Holt, 1943.

Middlebrook, Martin, *The Battle of Hamburg*, Charles Scribner's Sons, 1988.

Middlebrook, Martin, *The Berlin Raids*, Penguin, 1990.

Middlebrook, Martin, and Chris Everitt, *The Bomber Command War Diaries*, Penguin, 1990.

Middlebrook, Martin, *The Nuremberg Raid*, Penguin, 1973.

Moyes, Philip, *Bomber Squadrons of the R.A.F. and Their Aircraft*, Macdonald, 1964.

Overy, R. J., *The Air War 1939-1945*, Stein & Day, 1980.

Price, Alfred, *Battle Over the Reich*, Ian Allen, 1973.

Robertson, Bruce, *Lancaster--The Story of a Famous Bomber*, Harleyford, 1964.

Rust, Kenn C., *Ninth Air Force in World War II*, Aero, 1967.

Saward, Dudley, *"Bomber" Harris*, Cassell, 1984.

Sawyer, Tom, *Only Owls and Bloody Fools Fly at Night*, William Kimber, 1982.

Searby, Air Commodore John, *The Bomber Battle for Berlin*, Airlife, 1991.

Simmons, Kenneth W., *Kriegie*, Thomas Nelson and Sons, 1960.

Smith, Major General Dale O., USAF (Ret), *Screaming Eagle*, Algonquin Books, 1990.

Stiles, Bert, *Serenade to the Big Bird*, Bantam, 1984.

Verrier, Anthony, *The Bombing Offensive*, Macmillan, 1968.

In this, our perspective of the Allied bomber crew experience in World War II England, we offer a representative selection of the people, places, and events that made up that experience. It was not our intention to provide a comprehensive coverage of personnel, squadrons, groups, stations or commanders. We hope that *Round the Clock* conveys a sense of what it was like to be a bomber crewman in that time and circumstance.—*The authors*